Fate and Good People Kept Us Alive

A Family Memoir of Survival

By Regina and Stanley Zektzer

Fate and Good People Kept Us Alive
A Family Memoir of Survival

Published by
Magic Books
Edison, New Jersey

All of the photos used in this book are from the collection of the family of Regina and Stanley Zektzer

With Special Thanks to my brothers
Marvin Zektzer
Morris Zektzer

And special acknowledgment to Paul Greulich, for interviewing
and documenting the account of my mother's story.

To:

Mom- Regina Zektzer
Dad – Stanley Zektzer
Grandma Chaya (Clara) Brottman Koplowitz
All the relatives I never met who were killed before I was
conceived

IN MEMORY OF OUR PARENTS
MORDECHAI AND PEREL DINA ZEKTZER·MOISHE AVRAHAM BROTTMAN
SISTERS BRACHA·CHANA·RIVA
PERISHED IN THE HOLOCAUST

Our father, Stanley Zektzer's headstone. It also honors his
parents, brothers and sisters, and his wife's father, who died in
the war and have no graves or headstones to mark their passing.

Foreword

As I was compiling the stories for this book, typing out my father's hand-written story and watching his home made videotaped story of his life, listening to recordings of my mother talking about her experience, I was struck by their tremendous courage, ability to survive and what it took for them to come to a new country, where they didn't speak the language, look for jobs, find their way to a new life, learn to trust again, raise a family, make a living, and keep going!

My mother was more talkative about her experience during the Holocaust and when she spoke, she always credited her mother, my Grandma Chaya (Clara). My mother would talk about how Grandma was shrewd, always thinking ahead, planning their next move, always keeping the kids occupied, asking what day it was, she'd have them practice counting and reminding them about holidays. My grandmother was a survivor. She was the original pioneer woman. She was protective and never let anyone fall behind. She was smart and strong, and she instilled those traits in my mother and my uncles.

My father was less talkative about his time during the Holocaust. When he spoke, it was about how he felt leaving his parents and his beloved town, riding his bike out of town with tears in his eyes, all the while knowing it was time to leave; but not knowing when he'd be back and what he would find when he could return. His stories of growing up and the heart felt feelings about his town and the simple life they lived are best reflected in the poem he wrote, "I Long", found at the end of this book. His escape from Poland took him to countries far from the war, and his education and language skills were some of his most helpful tools. It wasn't until I began documenting his story from his written account that I realized ALL that he had been through.

While my parents both came from Poland, their experiences were very different. Each extremely difficult, each unimaginable and each powerful in their own way. What's profound though, is that through all it, they found a way to survive, found each other and found a way to start their journey to a new life, together.

Together they found their way to America, learned to speak English, secure work, save money, have a family, buy a farm and LIVE! Together they continued to move forward, surrounding themselves with friends from 'the old country' whose accents and stories were familiar, and new friends who accepted them, guided them and helped them learn new ways.

This book is not just their memoir, but a documentation of their stories of survival. It is intended to honor my parents, their siblings, and their parents. It's intended to serve as a documented family history for generations to come.

Paula
May 12, 2025

Part 1
Life Before the War

Chapter 1
Stanley

Kostopol… my little town; the place where I lived my first 19 years with my family.

Kostopol, my little down the home where I spent all of my youth, so happily.

I remember 1941, when war forced me to leave my home.

My eyes begin to fill with tears as I recall those youthful years in Kostopol.

Every day I used to play with the kids in the street, climbing trees, playing ball and even fighting with each other.

My name is Shloime, better known by the name Stanley Zektzer, and I'd like to tell you a story, it is the story of my life in the shtetl, the little town in Eastern Poland where I lived until Germany attacked Russia in June 1941, and forced me to flee my home, leaving my parents and sister and the entire family behind me, never to see most of them again.

It was a cruel war, and a holocaust in which six million of our people perished. Luckily, Eveyln and I survived, along with my sister Lillian, who left Poland in1939 before the war started. We all took root in America and managed to raise families.

***

On the Eastern side of pre-war World War II Poland, close to the Russian border in the area known as Wolinia, lay a small town named Kostopol. Thick forests surrounded the town from all three sides, leaving the southwest more open. There were fertile fields that yielded food for the area. The supply of water was plentiful. The main river, Goryn, with its tributaries that flowed through the area were a source of freshwater fish of all kinds—an excellent source of food. This area is now part of the Ukraine, the breadbasket of Europe. The ground is rich and fertile and not only supports its inhabitants but supplies crops to be shipped to distant regions of the world.

This good supply of grain and the thick forest helped in the development of a large lumber industry and the building of a large lumber mills and flour mills, where many of the local people found steady employment.

***

The beginning of the town of Kostopol can be traced to 1792, when the local Polish king Stanslav Poniatowski gave the area as a present to his officer Leonard Vurtiel, who was in charge of the supply of beef for the Royal Court. By the year 1864 Kostopol had a population of 607; 227 were Jewish.

There were six taverns owned by Jews with large families. They were concentrated in the area between the main road and the river that flows through town. Around these taverns, the Jews of Kostopol built their homes and formed the first street. Next to that street was a large open area, where the farmers gathered once a week to sell their produce. A synagogue was built. It was soon replace by a new building.

By the mid-nineteenth century, the Jewish community of Kostopol was in need of a shochet (ritual slaughterer) and that is the time when my grandfather, Rabbi Shlomo Shochet arrived in Kostopol. My grandfather was born in1830 and came to town with his wife as a young couple. They raised a large family of twelve children, most of whom married in town and contributed greatly to the growth of the Jewish community.

My grandfather was a zealot in religious matters and soon became the spiritual leader of early Kostopol. He was in charge of the building of the first synagogue and the ritual bath, which was a must in a Jewish community. Old timers told of how my grandfather raised money for maintaining the synagogue in his own way. On Saturdays after the service my grandfather would lie down on the door sill and not permit the worshippers to get out of the synagogue unless they left their 'talis' (prayer shawls) inside. During the week, when they came to redeem their tallit, they were asked to make a donation to the synagogue. He earned the greatest respect from the townspeople, and he accomplished what was needed to maintain Jewishness in the community.

From that first street, known as the Public Bath street, early Kostopol began to spread, first along the river and then across the main road, later known as the Highway Street, to form other streets. By the turn of the twentieth century, there were streets on both sides of the main road. The Jewish community grew quickly, and relations with non-Jewish neighbors were good in spite of hostile treatment that the Czarist Russia gave the Jews.

My father, Rabbi Mordachi Zektzer (also a ritual slaughterer) was born about 1885. He married my mother, Pearl Dina, the youngest daughter of my grandfather Shlomo Shochet.

My father was 18 and my mother was 21 when they married about 1903. They lived along the river where most Kostopol Jews lived at that time. But after a fire in the town, my grandfather, my parents, and my mother' sister Gisia and her family, went together to buy the largest home in town. It was on the road to the city of Ruvno, called later Ruvno Street, and was later filled with Jewish homes.

My father came from a town named Goshtcha, some fifty to sixty kilometers from Kostopol. Also, a son of a shochet (ritual slaughterer), he came from a larger family, four brothers, and two sisters. The two sisters later lived in the Ukrainian city of Charkow (Russia) and the brothers married in the area of Ruvno and built their families there. One brother, Yosel, lived in Goscha and was the shochet in town, Yechiel lived in Ruvno; Mojshe and my father in Kostopol and vicinity. We were closest to Mojshe who was nearby.

When my grandfather Rabbi Shlomo was ripe in years and could no longer perform the ritual slaughter of cattle, his two sons-in-law: my father and Leib, Geisia's husband, were put in charge. The Jewish community of Kostopol grew and Kosher meat had to be plentiful. There was more work for the shocha team and my uncle Leib married off his daughter Reize to a shochet who became a part of the clergy in Kostopol.

It was a Jewish tradition that once a position of a clergy in the community was established, it became that family's sole right to it and was passed on in the family. This is why my grandfather made sure that as he got old, his two sons-in-law would carry on in the Jewish tradition.

***

My grandfather Rabbi Shlomo made sure his family continued to lead the old synagogue which he had helped build. As he grew older, my father took over and became the Cantor. When the new synagogue was built next to the old one, my grandfather made sure that his son-in-law, Leib, would be in charge of that synagogue.

As the town grew, more homes were built. Because of the railroad station, Kostopol attracted many Jewish settlers from the nearby towns and villages. There were also Polish and Ukrainian settlers. Most of the Ukrainians lived near their church; the Poles were further on Highway Street and around the Jewish cemetery, where more streets were built.

The First World War in 1914 brought a halt to the growth of the town. During the four years of the war the Jewish population suffered as various armies occupied the town. First the Germans, then the Russians, then bands of Petluira, Denikin and again the new Red Army. Finally at the end of the war in 1918, the town became part of new republic of Poland until the Russians marched in in 1944and annexed it to the Soviet Ukraine.

It was a new beginning for Kostopol. The people learned the Polish language and adopted the system of the new Poland, eventually participating in elections to the parliament and local government and also governing the Jewish community. This was a new experience for the Jews of Kostopol who lived all their lives under the Czarist Russian regime.

It was a really new beginning!

Chapter 2
Regina

My name is Regina Zektzer. I come from a little town in eastern Poland called Zbarazh, near the Russian border. I'm the oldest of four children and the only girl. Zbarazh was like any other small village, small basic homes, people doing odd jobs, working fields, bartering. No office buildings, no modern conveniences, just basic country living, far from the next town. Life was simple and we only knew of world events from travelers who came through and shared stories.

As the oldest of four children and the only girl, I was expected to help with "women's work," washing dishes, preparing the meals, and helping around the house. Friday night was always special, it's the Sabbath and so we'd prepare soup, chicken and challah bread. A very traditional Jewish home, we would light candles and my father was the head of the house. We all followed his lead.

Life in town was simple, we had no electricity, no cars, everyone had a horse and a wagon, no paved roads. There was a small, one-room schoolhouse where all the children in the area attended and learned together. In school, I was very good at math and I was a very good student.

My mother ran a small general store near the train station where we sold coal. That's where I learned a lot about people, business, and how to handle myself with adults.

My brothers, all younger than me were typical boys; they were annoying, loud, and always bothering me! I didn't have dolls to play with, in fact, play was not really something we thought about. We cleaned up around the house, learned to cook and bake, went to school, and learned to behave. For girls, it was all about being a good "balaboosta" (housekeeper), so you could grow up, find a husband, get married and have a family. In fact, EVERYTHING was about family.

My mother was a stout, short but strong woman. Today we would call her a "pioneer woman." She took charge of her life, not letting anyone or anything get between her and her kids. She wore long black skirts and simple button down blouses with a short cardigan, boots and tights in the winter, and often a kerchief on her head. Women in those days mostly covered their hair partially a Jewish/religious rule, and partly because taking a shower or bath happened once a week—at the bathhouse! We didn't have fancy bathrooms, we basically had an outhouse, and once a week we went to the bathhouse with the others in town. No privacy at all, but that was the accepted way, and no one thought anything of it.

My mother was shrewd. Maybe from her days as a businesswoman, I'm not sure but she was clever, always thinking ahead. She could read people better than anyone.

We didn't have a phone, TV or even a radio. We played in the street, if we had time to play, with sticks and rocks, cans or whatever we could find. We found ways to get creative. I don't remember any crime. Everyone knew each other and there was a lot of respect for others' property and family. There were no cars; people rode horses or drove a horse and wagon.

Preparing the Friday night dinner was an all-day ritual. Mom would knead the dough for the challah, braid it and then put a lovely egg wash over it, then set it in the coal fired oven to bake. I learned early on how to braid a challah, and I remember how the dough felt sticky but not too wet, just the way my mother taught me. We'd knead the dough, then put it in a bowl to let it rise, covered with a kitchen towel. When it was ready, we would roll it, braid it and bake it, the aroma was delicious! The smell of baking challah, chicken soup, and chicken was the best part of the week. They would kill the chickens in the back yard then pull the feathers right there!

Chapter 3
Stanley

The first child in our family was my sister Bracha, who was born in 1905. A couple of years later my sister Hanna was born and my family, my grandparents and Uncle Leib and his family moved to the newly acquired home on the Ruvno Street. It was the largest in town and had twelve rooms. Through the length of the house was a corridor with a door on each side, and every room had a door to the corridor. Apparently, it was meant to be a hotel or perhaps it was just four apartments, for there were four kitchens. To make room for my grandparents, another room was added to my parents' apartment.

Beneath our house was a cellar which was as big as half the house, the walls made of red brick and a dirt floor. The few small windows never gave enough light and made the cellar very damp. This cellar was a storage place for all perishable foods, including dairy products, meat, pickled cucumbers, cabbage and others. Refrigeration was not available at the time but when necessary, chunks of ice chopped out of the river during the winter and buried under a mound of sawdust thru the summer, helped the process of freezing when the need arose.

The cellar beneath our home served also as a shelter for many of the town Jews, when during the first world war, the town was occupied by bands of Ukrainians, Russians, Germans and other armies. The cellar also served as a slaughterhouse for chickens, until in later years, a special building was erected for that purpose in our backyard.

***

In the new home my sisters Rivka and Lea were born. My sister Yochevet (Evelyn) was born during the First world War.

My grandfather outlived his wife by several years and in 1920 at a ripe age of 90, he left this world, leaving the task of maintaining Kostopol Kosher in the hands of two competent sons-in-law, my father and uncle Leib.

I was born January 19, 1922, in the new republic of Poland

and named after my grandfather Shlomo, the only son in the Jewish family after five girls was the happiest moment to my parents. It called for a celebration and most of the town's Jews were invited to the Bris. Everybody in our large house played with me. But soon this happiness would be clouded by disaster.

In 1924 at the age of two, I was stricken with polio, which affected my left leg. I had a series of treatments, doctor visits, and whatever could be done at the time. My parents were terrified, but I was lucky. The damage to my leg was not that bad and I continued to develop as normal as all the other children my age.

At this time, three rooms of our big house were rented out to a teacher and his family, and one room of this apartment became a school. It was in this one room school that I began my schooling in the Hebrew language, and later the Polish language.

I was about four years old when I was introduced to the Hebrew alphabet and at the age of five, I was fluent in the prayer book. Because the school was in our home, I was always the first one to come in, many times, while our teacher was still in bed! This teacher was very capricious and quite often would hit us or pull our ears for not obeying or not learning well. We were especially afraid of his famous belt, that his wife had in the kitchen, and when he would call out to his wife "give me the belt," we were petrified!

But we learned well, in spite of the fact that we were beaten many times. We couldn't complain to our parents because they were on the teacher's side. His method of introducing to use the Hebrew language was from posters that he printed, and then the prayer book. He also had advanced classes for older children, who were studying history and Bible. At that time Kostopol did not yet have a regular Hebrew school. Private one room schools, were the only source of Jewish education.

There were in town already several Polish government schools, separate for boys and girls. Education in public schools was compulsory, but also the private one room Hebrew Schools were legalized at the time. My sisters Evelyn, Lea, and Rivka attended the Polish school and learned Hebrew in the afternoon in private school. There were also Hebrew classes in public schools, where Jewish children learned Hebrew and Bible.

The children had to attend the public schools on the Sabbath, since schools were open six days a week. My father was instrumental in forcing the school authorities to allow the Jewish children to attend only as "listeners" on the Sabbath but not to do any writing, which in some way, solved the problem.

In 1927 my sister Bracha married and the wedding was the talk of the town. The groom, my brother-in-law Mojshe, came from a town called Stepan, about 35 kilometers from Kostopol and on the wedding day, we rode out in a wagon to meet the groom and his party on the outskirts of town. I remember well how the groom was placed in a neighbor's home across the street until the Chuppa (canopy) time, for it was forbidden for the groom to see the bride before the Chuppa.

It was Friday afternoon, as the wedding procession started to move from our house toward the synagogue, led by a band of musicians and the other children and I ran in front of everybody. Hundreds of spectators assembled in the synagogue yard to watch the Chuppa ceremony and then the processional marched back to our home to begin the festivities, which lasted the entire week.

When my sister and her husband left our home to take residence in their house in Mojshe's town, I wanted to go along. I accompanied them in the wagon to the outskirts of town, but cried a lot not wanting to leave the wagon until my sister bribed me with candy and I returned home.

The night before my sister Bracha and her husband left, a fire broke out in a neighbor's barn. The barn was full of straw and as the fire broke through the roof, the entire street was full of clusters of straw that flipped through the air. We packed our belongings and were ready to evacuate the house if it caught on fire. The street was full of people assisting the firemen to carry pails of water until the barn burned to the ground and the fire was out. Luckily, no other house caught fire and people went to bed, relieved that the houses were spared. This fire forced my father and uncle to replace the roof of the house, which was made of wood shingles, with a metal roof that would never catch fire.

The firemen did their job with great difficulties. First of all they were not professionals because the fire company was just formed and the equipment was primitive. Although they wore nice shiny brass helmets, the rest of the equipment was crude. There was a big pump drawn by horses, that was manned by eight men pushing a bar on each side, up and down to operate the pump. There were other wagons that had a tank of water drawn by horses, serving as a water reservoir, and if needed, they dug wells that many houses nearby added for a short time to supply water, although they were quickly drained. But little by little the firemen learned the art of fighting fires and in later years until World War II, there were no major fires in town.

But when occasionally there was a fire somewhere, the streets were full of people who ran as spectators or coming to help carry water or assist in saving the belongings of the house.

These early years of my life were spent around the home, in the street, where with other children my age we just played. Since there was almost no traffic in the street, we safely played on the road, which was not paved yet, either in the mud and sand or in the winter we played in the snow.

There was lots of winter equipment, sleds, skis and skates that were made. They were crude but served the purpose of having fun with them and because in that area the winter snow lasts about four months there was a lot of time to enjoy it.

But even in the spring and summer we had fun on the road, first to dig shallow ditches directing the water from the melting snow and in the spring, going barefoot in the street that was full of water, especially after a heavy summer rain.

Our street, like other streets in town, remained unpaved until early 1930 and when the snow melted in early spring the mud was terrible. The wagons sank into the mud. We children had fun watching the struggle.

It was better during the winter months when the road was snow packed, and all transportation was done by sled. During the winter, logs from the forest were brought to the plywood factory by sleds, and we had great fun to hang on to the logs to get a free ride, but we had to watch for the whip that the driver held in his hand! The most fun was building a snowman. We threw snowballs, smashing windows occasionally and getting beat up by our father.

It was a must to go with the father to the synagogue on Sabbath day and I especially had to go to the synagogue because my father was the cantor. While in the synagogue, I learned to help my father sing the prayers and at the age of five, I made my debut as a singer.

Kol Nidrei, at the conclusion of the service my father put me on a stand, and I led the congregation in singing Adon Olam, an upbeat and fun song that involves clapping along. From the balcony my mother's face was shining as all the women praised my signing.

That Yom Kippur might have been one of the happiest moments for my mother. My singing Adon Olam and Kol Nidrei became a tradition in our synagogue, and lasted until my Bar Mitzvah, when I felt I was too old. But now I sat near my father during the High Holidays, and learned his melodies, while helping sing along in the congregational singing. A boy in those days was not permitted to conduct services, so I just learned the cantorial skills.

While my father was not paid a regular salary for being a Cantor, on the eve of Yom Kippur, he and other chairmen of various committees sat in the synagogue at a long table and collected the money that every worshipper brought in as payment of their obligation. It is interesting to know that the majority paid their debts promptly before Kol Nidrei, to comply with the tradition to pay all debts before Kol Nidrei night.

Throughout the Yom Kippur day, I watched my father chant the liturgy, while the synagogue was packed to capacity without air conditioning, literally sweating it out without complaint. He believed wholeheartedly in what he was doing, knowing well that he was delegated by the congregation to intercede on their behalf with the Creator. I did not at the time even dream that someday in America, I would follow in my father's footsteps.

By the late 1920s, Kostopol was developing in a rapid pace, new homes were being built, and the Jewish community was growing fast. The factories in town attracted workers, many of them Jewish and the business district grew. Ninety percent of all stores in the district, numbering about 125, were Jewish, which in later years brough the rage of the Poles in town. But for the moment in these years, there was no problem, and the Jews were the businesspeople in town.

In 1928 the modern Hebrew school TARBUT, opened its doors, introducing modern Jewish education. The instructive language was Hebrew with Sephardic pronunciation (Spanish). And all subjects including mathematics and physics were taught in Hebrew. The Polish language was taught as a foreign one, including Polish literature.

I was enrolled in this school in 1929 into the third grade, because I had been taught in the one room school and was already well versed in Hebrew and some Polish. Soon thereafter, I also joined the Zionist scout organization, *Hashomer Hatzair*, where the love for the land of Israel was instilled in us. In this organization, I learned discipline, to get along with other children outside of the school walls, responsibility to carry out duties of the organization, and to eventually assume the role of leadership when the call came.

At this early age, we had no political motives and all activities centered on scouting. The winter months were spent inside playing games such as ping-pong, checkers, chess. Meetings were held once a week. During the summer we were busy with soccer games, outings in the forest, the beach, and camping.

The best place to play soccer was the large area near the Synagogue, which was used as a market for vegetables and other products once a week on Tuesday and the rest of the week was empty. The ground was hard packed, straight and in the middle of town, near our homes. A professional stadium was later built in the forest nearby. But for us, the area near the synagogue was good enough and even some gardens near our homes served our needs to play.

Because our organization was Zionist, and the most important campaign to raise money for the Land of Israel was the Jewish National Fund, abbreviated in Hebrew KKL—*Keren Kayemet LeIsrael*—we took part in that campaign. Every Jewish home in town had the familiar blue & white box where money was collected and emptied once a month by a group of volunteers. As children, we were not in charge of collecting the money from the boxes, but we did play a part on Chanukkah, and especially *Purim.*

It was a tradition for the Zionist organization in Kostopol to send out a group of youngsters during *Purim,* to stage a short *Purim* play at the homes in town to collect money for Israel. This event was fun because as we entered the homes, usually in the kitchen, there were so many goodies, *Purim* pastries *"Hamantashen,"* always freshly baked and we were either given or we helped ourselves.

Our play was the story of Joseph who was sold for a slavee to Egyptians by his brothers, and I played the role of Jacob, who was sending his son Joseph to the fields to see what the brothers were doing. I liked the story and enjoyed playing that role. There was no fun walking the streets of our town in the night of *Purim.* With the snow melting the street was full of mud and we were in it while making our way from house to house. But we raised money for Israel and that was the reward.

Another project to raise money for the Jewish National Fund was to sell empty bottles for two cents per piece, which was at the time a lot of money. One day, one of our group suggested that at the bottling company in town, there were lots of empty bottles in the yard and if one of us jumped the fence he could hand over the bottles and then we could come back to the owner of the bottling company and sell him the empty bottles. We did just that, but did not know that one of the owners saw us stealing bottles and when we came in with bottles, each of us holding a few, he said he would buy them. He told us to line up, then took each of our hats, that we had to wear always, and sent us home. It would have been a disaster to come home without a hat, so we begged him to forgive us, promising that we would never steal bottles from him. Eventually he gave us our hats and we left. We NEVER stole bottles again!

Chanukkah was fun. We played dreidel, for money, and there was no school for eight days, and with heavy snow, we had so much to do outdoors. But we also had an evening for latkes, and to that everyone had to bring supplies and even wood for the stove. When we ran out of wood one year, we broke up a nearby fence and used some of the boards for firewood. All that was in fun, and at the age of ten to twelve it was always an adventure.

Stanley's grandfather, Mordechi, and granddaughter Lillian at about three years old. He was about 90 when he died. Family stories said he made money by chiseling headstones for people who died, and he was lying in the cemetery doing that work, caught pneumonia and died.

Chapter 4
Regina

We had to make our own butter; we'd churn it and eventually you had butter.

There was a saying, "I feel like a goose before the slaughter." That meant someone had eaten too much. Many people in the area raised geese for food, and by September we would keep the geese in a pen and feed them a lot. We'd literally stuff food down their throats so they would get fat, we'd give them a lot of water and this went on for a few months. By December, it was time to kill the geese for food. The fat they had put on was pulled and put into a pot, boiled down and then used as a spread. We loved fried onions in fat or just used as a spread on bread. Most importantly, we'd save the grease to use at Passover as a fat. It would cook in the pot, and we'd store it in the basement where it was cool.

I was born in 1928, nearly ten years before the war that would bring such suffering to our country and the world. The national boundaries of Europe have been drawn and re-drawn many times, and today the town of Zbarazh is located in Western Ukraine.

During my childhood in the 1930s, Zbarazh was a simple community without paved roads. If you saw an automobile in our region of Poland, it was considered a novelty. We had no electricity or running water. Everyone had a winter basement for storing food during the colder months. All our food was natural, but it was only available on a seasonal basis. The town had a large Jewish population of about 3,000 people. One of the highlights of life came once a week when merchants gathered to set up booths to sell and trade their wares. There were old tunnels under the town that dated back to the time of the Tatars, a Turkic ethnic group. Sometimes children would explore these tunnels with their teachers, but I never took an interest in them.

My father Moses worked in real estate, brokering land purchases between people. He was a tall steady man with a nice way. I remember he used to drink tea from a glass and would put a sugar cube between his teeth when he drank the tea. Eventually the doctor told him he could not put the sugar cube between his teeth, he probably was diabetic, but no one knew what that meant.

My mother Clara, a stout short woman who was very serious, she often wore a kerchief around her head. The women always covered their heads, especially on the sabbath. She wore long skirts, a basic blouse and an apron. She would cook delicious meals like chicken soup with garlic and chicken feet (pitchha), helzel (stuffed derma). On Friday nights she would prepare the Sabbath dinner complete with chicken soup, chicken, and challah, a heavy, egg-based bread. Challah, braided, baked to perfection and always delicious. She taught me how to knead the dough so it was elastic and stretchy but not too wet, and then how to roll it out and braid it. To finish, she would prepare an egg wash, brush the challah and then bake it in the oven. The smell of fresh challah would fill the house on Friday and the aroma would bring all of us kids home for dinner. It was expected that everyone was home for Friday night dinner. It was TRADITION!

Clara was shrewd and an excellent judge or character; nothing got past her. She ran a grocery store located in the rear room of our house. It was more like a general store because the peasants could not easily travel to the city to buy goods. Our store sold items such as kerosene, sugar, and cigarettes. She and her sister exported coal.

When I was seven years old, I worked behind the counter with my mother. It was early practice, because many years later I would also find myself in a family business.

Chapter 5
Stanley

There was a great convention of the organizations of *Hashomer Hatzair*, in 1933, marking the 20th anniversary of its founding. Delegates from the Eastern part of Poland gathered to a little town named Selishtch, about 12 kilometers from my town. Our chapter sent a large group to the convention and I was in it.

The road was sandy and the horse was not able to pull the wagon, so we had to go part way on foot and partly in the hay packed wagon, one on top of the other, singing and having fun. We slept two nights in a grainery on top of stacked fresh hay. We marched through the village, sang at night around a bonfire, listened to speeches and had more fun. We met children our age from nearby towns, with whom we kept in touch with for years until 1939 when the Russians occupied the area, and our organization was dissolved.

Summer at these early years of my life was fun in other areas too. We had several ways to pick apples and pears and not to be caught. We used a big pole with a bent nail at the end and lay on the roof of our barn to pick pears. For apples, we had to jump over the fence and get to the first tree. The owner was almost blind, and his wife was almost deaf, so they could not hear or see what was going on. This orchard was so famous that children from all parts of town came to steal fruit. A lot of the fruit we gathered were small and hard, so we put them in fresh hay in the barn, for some weeks, and later took them out ripe and very tasty.

Many people in town kept a cow for milk, usually housed in a barn on their property. We also had a cow, which was a sometimes a problem for my mother, who was in charge of milking. At the beginning of 1930, my mother's health wasn't too good, and we needed someone to tend to the cow. This was done by a gentile woman who lived nearby and performed many chores for us, like firing the stove on the Sabbath, helping in the vegetable garden, and other jobs. During the summer, a shepherd boy would gather all the cows in the street early in the morning and walk them to the pasture outside of town. At night the cows returned home. Every cow knew his home and how to get back to the barn. As children we had great fun watching the cows return home from the pasture.

In 1930, the Rabbi of the town died and his brothers, since he was single, brought another Rabbi to take over for his duties. This was in line with Jewish tradition, that gave the family the right to do that. The new Rabbi was associated with the old Synagogue, where my father was the cantor, and the *shocahteem* (my father, uncle and his son-in-law) sided with the new Rabbi. But as it usually happens among Jews, there was a section in town, by the Railroad street, which opposed that new rabbi. They brought in another Rabbi for their synagogue and that sparked a conflict that lasted until the Russians occupied our town. That rebellious section of the town also brought in another ritual slaughterer to compete with my father and the rest of the *shochateem.* This was completely against Jewish tradition to intrude on a clergy position and it further divided the community. The slaughterer was also not permitted to perform anything other than just to slaughter chickens for that section of town that sided with his Rabbi.

The 1930's were very strenuous to my family. Our income was reduced first because the grocery store that we owned was closed by 1931, and second the intrusion of the new slaughterer. At the same time, my sisters Lillian and Rivka studied in Vilno, and soon Eveyln had to continue her education. My sister Hanna was in line to get married and this was not simple. My father wanted her to marry a *shochet*, so he would eventually take over my father's job.

The 1929 stock market crash in New York sent shock waves throughout the world and even in our small town, the crisis was felt. The town suffered financially, and my family was no exception. My father remodeled our store into three stores and rented them out, so we had some income from them. He also sold *taliseem* as a sideline, supplementing the income. We were generally comfortable financially but the greatest worry my parents had was to marry off Hanna. There was a process of looking for and introducing her to young men, until 1936 when she was married. By 1935 I was *bar mitzvah*, very simply just as all boys did in town. Because my father was the cantor, I learned the *Haftorah* and chanted it beautifully like no other boy.

In our town, usually boys did not chant *Haftorah*, the congregation read it, and the boy only sang the blessings. I was probably the only one that chanted the *Haftorah* and Blessings. After the service, the congregation was invited to our home for *Kiddush*, where I was asked by the Rabbi to again chant the *Haftorah*, from memory this time, and I did it really well.

I was now a teenager and because of our financial situation, could not continue with my education. A cousin of ours who had a leather goods store in partnership with others, asked me to be the cashier during the market days. I became a steady employee: a salesman, cashier, and many times ran the store while the partners took time off.

The time that we spent in those days was mainly in the Zionist organization, where we benefitted greatly both culturally and socially. There were hikes in the forest, meetings, games, and most evenings were spent playing ping-pong.

There was also the Main Street where in the evenings most youngsters congregated, walking the sidewalk singing, or just having fun. The movie house featured a new film once a week and that was a topic of conversation. We did not have, nor paid much attention to the radio, so books were important.

Once after seeing the moving *Frankenstein*, I walked home thinking of that monster, and passing the cemetery, I thought that I saw Frankenstein rising from one of the graves! I started to run home and as I entered the dark corridor, I turned to close the door and when I felt something push me inside, thinking it was Frankenstein, I jumped outside and saw a big dog running out of the corridor! I almost fainted!

Another interesting episode was in 1935, when the roof of the barn had to be replaced. Because there were many geese in cages in the barn, there was fear that thieves might steal them. The geese were raised for profit: fattened, slaughtered and sold. To make sure no one went to the barn at night while the roof was being replaced a guard was set up in the house, facing the barn. Taking turns, one of the men would sit in the house, looking out the window to see if everything was all right.

The night was clear and the moon was shining and my cousin—the *shochet*—was sitting at the window. He saw a man walking to the barn. He opened the door to the corridor and began yelling. We all woke up and stumbled into the dark corridor. Along the walls were obstacles like an old closet, a table, and other discarded furniture.

We finally made it to the back door and the balcony, still screaming while the thief began walking toward us. When he came closer we realized that it was a policeman just checking out the noise that the geese made. The policeman yelled at us, threatening to give us a ticket for disturbing the peace!

To our luck, he just went away, cursing the stupid Jews. In fact, the Polish police enjoyed mistreating the Jews whenever the occasion arose. Beginning in the mid-1930s, after Piilusdski's death, the Polish government became very antisemitic and the Poles in general followed the example. There was a campaign among the Poles not to shop in Jewish stores and in 1936 a bill to ban the ritual to slaughter cattle for kosher meat was introduced in the Polish parliament. There were restrictions placed on this ritual resulting in a cut of the supply of kosher meat. The young Jewish generation was disenchanted with Poland, and being very Zionist tried to get out of Poland and go to the land of Israel to build a Jewish homeland.

There were *Kibutzim* in our town, boys and girls who came from all parts of Poland, preparing themselves for communal living when they reached Israel. But Britain had a quota system, issuing only a certain number of visas yearly. If a boy received a visa for entry to Palestine he had the right to take along a wife and here was a chance to bring in more Jews to Palestine. My father, being a Zionist, helped greatly in this matter. He performed many fictitious weddings among those *Chhalutzim* (pioneers) who having those papers fooled the British entering Palestine and helping build the Jewish homeland.

My friends and I were involved in our Zionist organization getting prepared for the Kibbutz life and ultimately life in Palestine. I maintained my job in my cousin's store and had fun with my friends and especially the girls in our organization.

I was now a teenager, had discovered girls and was interested in some of them. At this age, most of the activities were in groups, either in our local or on the mail road in the evening. Stopping at a candy store or in the park. Since we were instructed in sex education in the organization at the age of thirteen or fourteen, there was much to talk about. We even had a night game in a field until morning, where after the game we sat around a bonfire, boys and girls and discussed sex education. This Zionist organization was a great source of knowledge for most of the activity was cultural.

Chapter 6
Regina

Our family had the help of a maid named Helena who scrubbed and dried our laundry outside by hand every Monday morning. For years Helena was our mother's right hand, and my mother cried when Helena got married and had to leave our employment.

My grandmother also lived with us. I had three younger brothers, Johnny, Paul, and Jack. Jack was the youngest, born in 1936. Paul was very responsible and studious. Johnny, however, often got into some form of trouble. Johnny didn't ride his bike so much as fly his bike. One day he broke his collar bone playing on a construction site in town. One of Johnny's mottos was, "Life comes first, school is second." These personalities would become clearer when tested by future hardships.

Paul was very tall, the second in the line of kids. He was smart, very good with numbers and books. Johnny was the wild one, he was a tough guy, always protecting the family and would later on, after the war, go on to play soccer for a Canadian team. In fact, when we came to the U.S., Johnny went to a doctor for anxiety, not sleeping and heart beating fast. Of course no one even thought of PTSD; it just didn't exist at the time. You were expected to just get on with life. But for him, he couldn't shake it. He saw a doctor for years who prescribed him pills and kept prescribing them for years.

My siblings and I had few luxuries, basic clothes that we wore sometimes for several days at a time, and simple shoes. The boys had two sets of black pants and white shirts that were constantly being washed because they wore these cloths to school and after to play. There was no electricity, no phones, no computers. We barely had paper and pens or books.

Like all kids, we spent time attending school, playing ball, and doing chores. The countryside was beautiful and flowered during the summer, and we enjoyed taking walks. I was something of a second mother to my younger male siblings and was often annoyed by their rambunctious nature. They outnumbered me and would tease me and drive me crazy sometimes.

Regina's mother Clara, and Clara's sister Shleema.Clara's Yiddish name was Chaya. The photos was taken about 1905.

Chapter 7
Stanley

In 1935, my sister Hanna got married to a shochet who became a partner in my father's half of the clergy position. This was given as a dowry as well as three rooms in the house that was part of our property. In 1936, my sister Bracha finally gave birth to her long awaited first child, a beautiful girl named Feigele (birdie). It was the first grandchild to my parents and to make it easy for my sister, she stayed with us the first month after the birth of the baby. But during the month, she developed a clot in her leg and when the local doctor was unable to do anything, he sent her to the city of Lvov, some 120 kilometers away. My sister Rivka went with her to Lvov and her husband Mojshe came along. Suddenly, on the first day of Rosh Hashana in 1936, a telegram came from Mojshe which said, "Father come immediately, pray to god!"

I was out with my friends during the day in the forest and coming toward evening I headed home and found everyone home and neighbors alike all crying. I was petrified of that all until I learned as to what happened. My father couldn't go on Rosh Hashana, since he was the Cantor so Uncle Mojshe, my father's brother went to Lvov to assist.

Bracha's clot began moving and bypassing the heart, went to her head and damaged her hearing. She survived the ordeal, one in a million, but was almost deaf and spent two months in the hospital. In the meantime, my mother cared for the baby until Bracha returned home. It was a hardship but Fiegele was beautiful and we all loved her. During those years of the mid 30s, my sister Evenly spent 1935 in a Kibbutz in Poland in the city of Chenstohova. She returned to Kostopol in 1937 saying a boy in the Kibbutz who was going to Israel would like to marry her and would come back to Poland to bring her, on his papers to Israel.

My father objected because the boy's father was a taylor and Eveyln wasn't decisive enough to go against our parents' wishes. She corresponded with the boy in the meantime hoping for a change.

My sister Lillian was away from home teaching Hebrew school in different parts of Poland. Returning home for vacation in 1937, she was introduced to a young man whose sister lived in Kostopol. The boy was teaching in a little town a distance away and he proposed that she come to teach there. Having no set plans for the moment, she agreed and after an interview was hired.

She started the new school year in that town where she and the boy, David, were the only teachers, and as usual a romance developed. The letters home did not indicate that there was anything serious but in 1938, one day she came home and said, "Tomorrow we are getting married, and we are going to Columbia, South America."

Upon learning that, preparations were made for the wedding the next day. Time was important because papers had to be filed with the Columbian Embassy. It turned out that some of the town's Jews were going to settle in Columbia on farms and in order to have a Hebrew teacher for their children, they offered David to come along, which he promptly accepted and suggested to Lilian to get married and come along, also.

While Lilian came home to prepare for the wedding, David went to his hometown some 40 kilometers from Kostopol to bring his sisters to the wedding. The wedding was called for 9:00 p.m., the next day but David missed the train and while everyone came to the wedding on time, the groom did not.

The next train was 12:30 AM. When the groom and his sisters came they just had enough time to walk in and go to the *chuppa*. The wedding proceeded as planned till early morning the next day. Lillian and David returned to teaching and awaiting formalities for the immigration to Columbia.

Now there was a new problem, sending money out of Poland for Lillian and her husband David. There was an expense for the immigration papers, travel, and others. My father worked hard to meet it all. Evelyn and Rivka were home and I was still a teenager working still at my cousin's store, earning money for my personal needs.

At this time I was very active in the Zionist organization, taking on leadership of a young group and at the same time reading a lot and self-educating. I spent a lot of time among my friends and usually every evening and weekends we would spend time at meetings or hikes in the forest nearby. In all our talks, we the teenagers of Kostopol dreamed of getting out of Poland and the way to do it was to go to a Kibbutz and prepare for life in the Land of Israel. In fact, in 1939 we already made plans to join a Kibbutz in a town near Vilno, one that was being formed by young people my age.

In the meantime, the political situation in Europe got tense. Germany was making demands on Poland. Germany had overrun Czechoslovakia, Hungary, and Austria and the world said nothing. Now Germany wanted territories from Poland, claiming that it was part of Germany. Jews were being driven out of Germany, prosecuted, killed, and those who did come to Poland told stories of horror. David and Lillian got permission to go to Columbia. Their departure from Kostopol was in July 1939, and I hoped that someday I would be able to perhaps go to Columbia and join them. By this time my father used up all the resources to send them out of Poland, so even I helped out with a 100 zlotys which I gave to David at the railroad station while waiting for the train to depart the city.

We had great hopes that now Lillian would be able to do something for us, from South America, but we did not know that Europe was on the brink of war.

Part Two
The War Comes

Chapter 8
Stanley

In the meantime, the political situation in Europe worsened, with the march of German armies into neighboring countries of Austria, Czechoslovakia and the word "war" was on everyone's lips.

The news from Germany was that the Nazi's were burning synagogues, robbing Jews of their possessions, and depriving Jews of all their rights. Germany made demands on Poland to hand over to them the "corridor," a portion of territory between Prussia and Germany. The Poles refuse. On September 1, 1939, the German Army crossed the Polish border and began their race east and World War II began.

Right from the start of the war, we knew that the chances for Poland to survive were minimal. During the last four to five years, Germans spies had penetrated the Polish government and the military, so at the outbreak of the War, the Polish army was not prepared and the small Polish Air Force was destroyed on the ground.

There was a call up of the reserves and some men in our town went out to war, but besides a blackout and some strafing by several German plans, our town was calm and life went on as before.

The radio boasted of victories and continued coded messages apparently to military units, which mean nothing to us in town. The Jewish population in our town was concerned, for we knew that Poland was being destroyed.

By Friday, September 15, Kostopol was full of refugees who came from mid and western Poland and told horrible stories of the war. Our street was jammed with cars who ran out of gasoline and hundreds of refugees, some on foot, some on bikes, all attempting to reach the Russian border, where it was thought the Germans would not come near.

There was great chaos among the Poles, fearing that the Polish Army would try to take a stand in Kostopol and fight hard, my mother, sisters, and neighboring women and children went to the village of Selisch as they had in World War I, some 21 years before, hoping to wait it out there.

My father, brother-in-law, myself, and other men remained home to guard our property. Among the many refugees who passed our home, my father spotted four Jewish boys, brothers, who came from Warsaw, and invited them to send shabbat with us. There was a great uncertainty and panic grew.

Sunday, September 17, 1939, rumors spread that the Russian army crossed into Poland and the Poles in town thought they were coming to help. Meantime the Plish army units who passed through our town forced merchants to sell their goods for vouchers that already had no value. Under threat of a gun they bought things and went on their way.

Toward evening, my mother, sisters and other neighbors returned from Selishch, and told of seeing along the way Russia units who told them they would be in Kostopol tomorrow. That night we waited to see what would happen.

*The Zektzer family. First row, left to right, Bracha (Stanley sister),
Pearl (Stanley's mother), Bracha's daughter, Faiglela, (translation,
little bird), Lea (in Yiddush, Laika and also know as Lillian),
husband David, Mordechai (Stanley's father), Evelyn (in Yiddush,
Yohevit) and Hanna (in Yiddush, Chana), Stanley's sisters). Back
row, Shumelic, Hanna's husband, Rivka (Stanley's sister), Aunt
Ziesel, Stanley.*

Chapter 9
Regina

When the war started, we didn't know what was happening, all we knew was that the Russians came and the Polish president made a big deal about Russia and Germany and an agreement they made with each other. For us, all of a sudden Russians came and for 18 months we were under Russian rule. We had to learn Russian letters. They are very different than Polish letters. For example the Russian R is the same as the Polish T- so it was a lot to learn and we were forced into it, but we were young and so learning came easy, at least to me, I loved going to school!

In fact, the teacher sent a note home with me one day, requesting that my mother come to school. My mother was upset with me. "What did you do?" she asked.

"Nothing I just did my work," I replied.

I was so scared that I was in trouble, and so my mother went to the school and saw the teacher. The teacher asked my mother, "So tell me who helped your daughter with her homework?"

"No one. Why? What did she do wrong?"

The teacher looked at her with disbelief. "Are you *sure* no one helped her?"

She continued to give my mother a hard time, swearing that someone had to have helped me.

"I remember my daughter was up late at night working on papers but I didn't know what they were about."

Finally, the teacher believed my mother.

Chapter 10
Stanley

Monday morning September 18, there was a rumble of armor, and as we ran to the main road, we saw a Russian tank pull up in front of the Police station and stop. Soon there were other military vehicles and personnel.

As the Polish police arrived at 8 o'clock for work, they were disarmed and their guns put in the middle of the road. Other military men that were in the area also disarmed and by midday a big pile of weapons were on the road and all the police officers assembled in the garden at the station.

Later on, they marched off apparently to be taken to Russia and were never seen again.

We were now under Russian rule and appeared to be of becoming part of Russia.

Life in town became normal and it seemed the Germans and Russians had agreed to divide Poland among themselves, so at this point the war was over and we became Russian citizens. The government ordered the stores to reopen but as goods were sold, nothing was replaced and soon the stores were empty and closed down. Because I was a salesman at my cousin's store, I became a leader in the Union of Salespeople and later given management of a supply store. Here I had a chance to get supplies for our family and also to help other friends.

Many institutions and offices were organized, and a Russian-Ukrainian high school opened where I enrolled immediately to learn the Russian language and to advance my education. It was an evening school and enabled me to work during the days.

Before engaging in work, I travelled with my father or brother-in-law to the city of Lvov many times, to bring slaughtered chickens which were not available there and sell them at a good price. We brought back liquors and textiles that we needed. This was a black market and if caught, was punishable by imprisonment. While we took our chance for a while, it soon became clear that the danger was great, and we stopped

I now took a job bookkeeping and spent much time between the office and school. I was one of six boys who entertained at the newly organized club in town. We sang Russian and Polish songs and even entertained at the polls on election day to the Russian Soviet Parliament in the winter of 1940. We were now living the Russian way; I'd mastered the Russian and Ukrainian languages and changed completely the outlook on life. The socialist systems were the way to go, where I thought everyone had a chance to achieve the most in life, not only the rich as in Poland.

In the spring of 1941, there were rumors that a German plane was shot down near Ruvno and the pilot taken into custody. Rumors persisted that the Germans were preparing for war. the large transports of troops and equipment that passed so often on the railroad was a good indication that something was coming. It was believable that the Germans, having signed a non-aggression pact with Russia, would never go to war.

In the meantime, my sister Hanna was preparing to give birth to her first child, so on June 14, 1941, she and her husband Shmuelic, took the train to Ruvno for the hospital where she would have her baby. Because the baby seemed to be coming prematurely Hanna remained in the hospital and Shmuelic returned for a few days home.

Chapter 11
Regina

When the war began in 1939, Hitler and Stalin made a pact to divide Poland in half. Poland's secretary of state was allegedly in cahoots with Germany's Nazi government. Germany attacked Poland from the West and Russia attacked from the East. The Germans seized our country's coal resources while the Russians took over the breadbasket, in the Ukrainian region.

Our brave soldiers were overwhelmed in about a month and Poland was occupied by foreign troops. The communist forces that took control of our region rounded up the wealthiest families and sent them to Siberia. In our town the local horse breeders met this fate. But this oppression paled in comparison to what lay ahead.

In September of 1941, Hitler stabbed Stalin in the back and attacked Russia. German troops overran the portion of Poland occupied by the Soviets, taking the whole country for themselves before continuing deep into Russia itself. When the Russians all ran away, we didn't know what happened. We were left to our own devices. In the beginning, when the Germans came it was the Wehrmacht, the regular soldiers.

Chapter 12
Stanley

At this time I was sent to Ruvno for a special course in bookkeeping so on June 20, 1941, Shmuelic and I went to Ruvno, where I had to make arrangements for the course while my brother-in-law was visiting with Hanna. It was Friday, and toward evening and in the home where we stayed we ushered in the sabbath. During the next day after attending shul, Shmuelic visited Hanna, while I had to attend to things at the office.

The evening of June 21, 1941, was clear and warm and the long wide Stalin Avenue was full of people enjoying a nice summer night. The restaurants were packed and in the few parks along the avenue, bands were playing, entertaining people who danced and had fun. Military personnel were all over the avenue. Dressed in their holiday uniforms, they enjoyed their evening off on a beautiful summer night. Nobody could have dreamed that in the early morning hours this same city would have a different look, that these same military men would no longer be happy, and there would be no more music in the parks.

This Saturday night I went to see a film about the war between Russia and Finland that had gone on for a short few months in the winter of 1940. I was very sad seeing all the casualties of that war.

It did not dawn on me that the next day, I too would become a victim of a terrible war, which was to kill 60 million people, including most of my family and changed Europe forever.

During the evening, Shumelic and I tried to communicate with Hanna but couldn't. She was apparently in labor and they did not let in visitors in the evening.

Over the telephone, the hospital told us that she had given birth, but we should come in the morning for more details. Those were the procedures, and we couldn't do any more, so we went home and fell asleep, hoping for good news in the morning.

About 4 a.m. I woke to the sound of gunfire, which appeared to be coming from Anti-Aircraft guns. I looked out the window and saw military personnel in the street, I took it as wargames and went back to bed.

By 6 a.m., there was shooting, and going outside I saw a lot of people in the street, confused as to what was going on. We also saw two planes in the sky apparently to whom the shots were directed. By now, the main avenue was blocked to traffic by military vehicles. This is not war games, but REAL WAR. Not until 9 a.m. did we learn from the radio, in a speech by Foreign Secretary Molotov, that a few hours before, without warning, the German Army crossed the border into Russia and was moving rapidly forward. Now it was official. WAR!

Shmelic and I went to the hospital to see Hanna; she had given birth to a girl and was feeling fine. We were still not permitted to see her but sent a note and she replied in a note that she knew it was war and she was worried. We sent in some goodies to her and assured her that things would be alright. We decided to return to Kostopol that day, and Shumelic would return to Ruvno in a couple of days to bring Hanna home.

During Sunday, June 22, 1941, the first day of War, German planes kept up the raids on Ruvno, dropping bombs here and there and creating a panic. It was not easy to reach the railroad station because of the bombardment and the shooting from low flying planes. We were forced to move alongside buildings, inching our way toward the railroad station.

Tickets were not being sold and when the train finally came, an hour late we hardly managed to get in through a window, because it was so full. There were people in doorways and there was no way to get onboard through the door. We never bought tickets and nobody could even check for tickets. Within an hour we were in Kostopol.

The town was in darkness and when we got off the train, a larger group of townspeople were waiting to hear the news from Ruvno and of the war. In our town, so far, everything was quiet. Shmuelic and I hurried home to tell the family the good news about Hanna and face together the problems that the war brought on. Everyone was worried about Hanna in the hospital in a city under bombardment. It was decided that Shmuelic would return to Ruvno

Tuesday to bring Hanna home.

Monday morning I went to the office to work as usual, but nobody had his mind on the books. Every day, German planes passed over the town but did not do anything. Men were called up to mobilize into the army, but after two days in the barracks, they were sent home for lack of transportation. There was great confusion and local government did not know what to do.

Shmuelic left Tuesday for Ruvno, but Wednesday, Ruvno was bombed very hard and people who escaped and reached our town told of great destruction and death. We heard nothing from Shmuelic and Hanna with their baby girl and only hoped that they would soon make it back.

In the meantime, my family began making plans. Things looked very bad and there was talk of crossing into Russia, hoping the Germans would never reach there. We were confident the Russians would make a stand at their old border and drive the Germans back. On Thursday, June 26, 1941, it became apparent that the Soviets were leaving the area, we began finalizing our plans to escape.

Friday, June 27, early in the morning, our street was already packed with Jewish men going on foot in the direction of the old Russian border, toward the town of Ludvipol. I quicky got dressed and went outside where I learned that the Soviet government had left our town, and the Germans were closing in. Nobody really knew what to do, but it was obvious that Jewish men should not remain in town.

By 6 a.m. many of our friends were in front of our home discussing what to do and quickly deciding to leave town; They urged me to come along. I could not decide to leave my home, parents and family, I, the long-awaited and only boy, to go away by myself into the unknown?

I talked to my parents, urging them to leave everything and come along – together – and not take a chance here. My parents' decision not to go was understandable. They had lived in Kospotal all their lives, built a home and raised a family and being older people, where would they go? Who would harm them here, they thought? Why would anyone harm my father who worked all his life, worked for Yeshivot, and helped the poor and the orphans, and the Jewish community in all areas. My folks felt that perhaps the young boys should leave; they would stay and as soon as the war ended, perhaps in a few weeks, we would return.

By now, my friends and most of the young boys in town had left for the Russian border and I soon realized that I was perhaps the last boy in town. The fear for the Germans was great and I soon decided to leave. I asked my sister Riva to pack clothes for me and I told my parents of my decision. Time was running out for me as I heard the thunder of big guns coming from the direction of Ruvno. It was obvious the Germans were closing in. Because it was Friday morning, my mother was preparing for the Sabbath, baking challah and special pancakes for breakfast. I was not in a hurry, so I took four hot pancakes for the road, a briefcase with candies and 200 rubles in my pocket, took out my bike, put on my backpack with clothes, the briefcase on the bike and was ready to leave.

Heartbreaking was my departure. In front of the house were my father, mother and the rest of the family, a few neighbors all with was such sad faces, crying as they said good-bye to me, not knowing what was in store for them, or me.

I'd never seen my father cry as he did now, even at the time when my sister Bracha's life was in danger. Afterall I was the long-awaited son after five girls!, and I was about to leave. Only GOD knew when, and if I would ever return home. Tears choked me and I could hardly say a word. After kissing everyone good-bye, I stepped on the bike, mumbled "Mom and Dad, I will soon return," and quickly took off, afraid to look back.

I turned into narrow Church Street, and soon was on the main road in the direction of Ludvipol, and the Russian border. In front of their huts along the road, the Ukrainians stood, happy seeing the Jews fleeing for their lives. Because the road was paved with cobblestones, my ride was bumpy and I used the path alongside that was softer for riding.

Suddenly, I thought that I didn't have socks in my backpack and decided to turn back. As I crossed over the road and started back, I soon realized how foolish it was to return home, and again, changed my route to go directly out of town. I rode quickly through the village and away from Kostopol hoping to catch up with all those who had left town just hours before.

About five kilometers from Kostopol, the paved road ended, and sandy road began. It was a hot June day and because it was impossible to ride a bike in the sand, I used a path in the forest along the road and soon caught up with my townspeople who were resting there. Ludvipol was 40 kilometers away and while it was very hot, walking required rest. To my sorrow my bike had a flat, so I was walking with a backpack and pushing my bike.

By mid-day, as I rested in the forest, it dawned on me that my sister Eveyln was in Ludvipol, where I was . That morning the family had been rushing so much we forgot about her. During the day the Ukrainians along the road refused to take our Russian rubles and we could hardly by food. Remembering that I would soon see Evelyn in Ludvipol, I walked more vigorously and toward evening arrived in the town where Evelyn was already waiting for me. Early arrivals of our townspeople had told her that I was on the road. It was Friday night and the Jews in Ludvipol brought in the sabbath as usual and in the house where Evelyn lived, I had a good Shabbat meal.

In the morning, more Jews arrived, some from Kostopol, and told us the Germans were close. We knew we must get over the border before it was closed. The border was perhaps 10 kilometers away and during the day, most of our townspeople head there. Evelyn and I decided to wait till evening when the director of the Office of the Forestry would order an evacuation, and we would go with them.

Late in the evening, the order came and immediately we began teaming up the horses in the dark, with five wagons each, drawn by two horses; three horses each were tied up for back-up. We moved out from Ludvipol in the dark, riding through the night. By morning, we reached the border. At a small wooden bridge a Russian soldier checked our passports and let us go through. We were in Russia!

Photos from Stanley's travel documents

Chapter 13
Regina

When the German's came to town, it was like magic! They drove big, fancy cars and they were shiny and clean. We learned that the Germans were taught to be immaculate and orderly. They wrote everything down and kept incredibly accurate records. Everyone was in awe, first by the cars, then by their uniforms, so crisp, pressed, and neat and clean! And their boots were shiny tall boots; we never saw anything like it!

It was impressive and scary, intimidating, and interesting. They were dressed very elegantly. everyone wore high shiny boots. We saw so many motorcycles with sidecars. We never saw so many trucks. It was the most mechanization we had experienced.

People told us the Germans were now occupying all of Poland, but the human mind struggled to accept that such a thing could happen.

Within a year of the invasion, the SS took charge of our village. The SS carried out the dreadful work of enforcing the Nazi regime's racial policies, including running the regime's concentration camps. When the SS came, things started changing. It began with verbal abuse. When you walked on the street, the SS would order you to go on the other side of the street, claiming that "Jews have lice and they carry disease." So, we had to walk on the other side so as not to infect others. Then the SS started beating up people. If you walked on the street with a beard they came and cut off the beard.

Any Jews older than age thirteen were ordered to wear an armband when out in public. These armbands were originally white and blue, but a few months later they were replaced by a yellow star worn on the chest. This form of identification was intended to be more visible at night.

Chapter 14
Stanley

At first glance, nothing changed once we crossed the Russian border, but soon we discovered, that the people in the villages were poor and the collective farms were no better off. They did not have sufficient bread for sale, but we could buy eggs and milk, that they did have.

Our destination was the superhighway to Kiev, where we could ride our wagons alongside on the dirt road which ran parallel to the highway. But here we were suddenly caught in a mine field, with guns and tanks camouflaged in the bushes, and it took the military some time to direct us to the highway and out of the mine field.

We were now riding alongside the superhighway on the parallel dirt road because it was too dangerous to get on the highway. The drivers of the trucks and other military vehicles that clogged the roads were half asleep and tired from long hours of driving and caused many accidents. Along the road lay dead animals killed by trucks, and smashed vehicles that no one had time to clean up. This was war and no one bothered with anything else.

As we approached Nouogrod-Volinsk, the first big Russian city we witnessed a dogfight overhead as German planes bombed the city. We watched the planes go after each other and saw the city burning after the bombardment. As we neared the city, we were stopped by the military who wanted us to get out of our wagons and help dig trenches for defense of the city.

The area was teaming with bulldozers, tractors, and tanks and only through the intervention of the director of our convoy, who presented the military with official papers that our convoy was needed in Kiev, they let us go on. When we arrived in the city, the fires were still burning and after buying supplies we continued to Zhitomir.

Toward evening, we approached Zhitomir and stopped in one of the streets for the night. I knew about this city from stories my father told from World War I and of a big Jewish population there. But before we had a chance to get out of the wagons and unhitch the horses, German planes attacked!

The sirens began wailing and people ran for shelter, but we had no place to hide. They would not let us in the bomb shelters, since we were strangers, and all strangers were suspects. We remained in the street, illuminated by the flares which the planes released. We hid under the wagons, hoping not to be hit by a bomb or bullet. It was a great spectacle, watching the color tracer bullets flying all over and when it was over, we fell asleep in the wagons until morning.

The city was peaceful when we woke up, but a conflict developed between Evelyn and the director, and Evelyn decided to leave the convoy and go alone to the train to Kiev. After talking to people in the city, we learned the next morning there would be a train ready to evacuate people from Zhitomir, and we decided to be on that train.

We took our belongings and walked to the railroad station where we stayed the night in the little park at the station, the only place that allowed passengers to use as a waiting place. This little park at the station was full of Zhitomir people, who hoped to be the first on the train.

The loading lasted throughout the day, with people shoving and screaming, all trying to get a better place in the freight cars. The train's destination was unknown, but it was going east, away from the battles and toward safety.

Toward evening we began moving, our freight car packed with women, children, and a few men, all sitting on their packages in the dark. There was a blackout during the war, and in the war zone, there were no lights at night, all windows had to be covered with black paper. But our car had no windows and for fresh air, we kept the sliding doors open a bit. During the night, one of the ladies fainted and the screams of the women were unbearable. Some men wanted to help but couldn't get close because the floor of the car was packed with people sitting on their baggage, so in the morning, the train was parked three kilometers from a railroad junction after a bombing raid on that city, it was decided to get off this train and walk to the railroad station and there get a local train to Kiev.

We took our packages and walked along the tracks to Kiev.

Chapter 15
Regina

Then they started putting Jews to work. This was largely just an excuse to punish them and put the fear of death into them. In our little town they killed a horse and needed ten people to bury the horse. So, my father who was a big man, and nine other men started digging. As they worked, the Germans beat the men mercilessly with rubber hoses. They finally dug the hole and I remember my father coming home that night and my mother taking out water and rags. On his back you could see every welt where they struck him. And of course, this abuse left us in a state of terrible fear.

People gradually forgot about their normal lives and started concentrating on how to survive. We did whatever work we were ordered to do. My mother and I worked too. Our job was to load wheelbarrows full of stones and bring them to the railroad tracks for construction work being done there. We concluded that the men had to hide because they were being punished mercilessly by the occupiers. Eventually, we learned not to venture outside at night. And then came a decree that we had to leave our homes and go into a ghetto.

Before the Germans came, we didn't even know what the word ghetto meant. The SS told us to take a horse and wagon and whatever you could fit on the wagon. Pots and pans, bedding, clothes. Those were the only possessions we were allowed to bring to the ghetto. The ghetto was located in our own town, next to a convent with a tall wall. It was always in the poorest part of a town or city. There were people there from many surrounding towns as well. Everyone was driven into one enclave, the ghetto. It was fenced in with barbed wire. They assigned us to live in a little house there.

The Ghetto was self-governing, so our own people were in charge and of course reported to the Germans. The first day in the ghetto, the German soldiers made rules. They said "we need ten kilos of silver, and if you don't give it to us, twenty-two lives will be lost."

Just like that!

Every household had a silver candelabra for sabbath candle lighting so the first few weeks everyone would give up their candelabras in hopes that they would spare lives of our friends and neighbors. The terror that went through the ghetto was indescribable, we were afraid every minute of the day. They kept us on alert changing the requirements of what they needed or wanted whenever they felt like it. A few weeks after the sliver request, they said we needed to give them gold, and if it was not delivered by the next day, sixty-four would die.

Now if you are governing the ghetto and you report to the German's but these are your people, your friends, neighbors maybe even family, how could you choose which sixty-four people would be sent to their death? That is how they controlled us with mind control, complete terror and fear. They turned us against each other so we could not trust anyone. Every day we'd wake up filled with fear of what the day would bring—death, starvation, beatings. What else could they do to us?

Then they came for furs. Everyone had furs; it was Poland! They came for furs to every house and whatever you had, you had to give it up. At that point, it was a small price to pay for one more day of peace and life.

The ghetto police were German and anything and everything went into their pockets. And children, well they went too. Soon, no one let their children outside to play—especially twins! Dr. Mengele, a monster in the camps, was experimenting with twins. He wanted to understand how twins were created how they relied on each other, so he experimented in ways I just cannot even verbalize.

He experimented with women who were pregnant, and going into labor, he'd tie their legs together and wait to see how long it would take for the baby to die. He allowed mothers to give birth, then see how long the baby would cry before it died, while keeping the mother strapped to the table.

Food was rationed. Sometimes you snuck out from the ghetto to the fence and the peasants came and gave you greenery and you traded it for whatever you had. If you were caught you were beaten. It happened to me once. I had vegetables hidden under my coat, and the guards took everything away and smacked me around and told me to go home. Children were discouraged from leaving their homes. Blonde children with blue eyes were known to be abducted and sent to Germany to be raised by childless Aryan parents.

We stayed in that ghetto from 1941 to 1943. We worked and tried to manage food and avoid punishment. My grandmother passed away in the ghetto at the age of 75. They did not allow me to go to the cemetery but as they carried the casket away, they opened it every few meters to prove there was a dead body inside and not someone trying to smuggle themselves out of the ghetto.

Chapter 16
Stanley

Kiev is capital of the Ukraine. My father told many stories of his travels there during WW1 and with the New Russian regime in 1939, we learned much more about the beautiful city. As we came out of the station, we saw nice clean streets with many nice buildings, especially the central business street, Kreshtchatic, quiet, elegant and beautiful. Electric buses kept the noise down. It was very serene.

We wanted to see a friend, Woloshyn, who lived nearby. He was a bookkeeper and had stayed in our home in Kostopol for a few months while working for the same office as Evelyn.

We met Mr. Woloshyn and his family, but he could not help us with anything because they were already preparing to evacuate since the frontlines were getting closer to his home. There was an air raid and we had to spend a while in the bomb shelter. Mr. Woloshyn advised us to go to the Botanic Gardens where all the refugees were gathered and to seek help there.

At the Botanic Gardens we took up residence under a tree among tens of thousands of others who came in every day. Here the government had free kitchens, where everybody got soup to stay alive and a little bread. This was a transition place and from here, everyday people left and went farther east away from the war zone which was moving closer and closer.

The German planes raided the city every day and night. We got used to the spectacle of rockets and tracer bullets, looking on from behind the trees. Evelyn went to the office of the Department of Forestry, where she was paid the salary that was due her. While there, she saw the Director, who was now getting ready to evacuate. He again invited Evelyn and me to join the convoy whose destination was Harkov, the second largest city in the Ukraine, 500 kilometers to the East.

We were so far from our home in Kostopol and getting farther away every day. We decided to join the Convoy again and on the evening of July 9, 1941, we began our long ride in the 5 wagons with 13 horses, slowly winding our way through the quiet streets of Kiev, toward the long bridge over the Dnieper river which passes through the city. The bridge was heavily guarded with balloons filled with explosives which were suspended high over the bridge to detour German planes. It took a while until we crossed over.

We later stopped along the road near a small forest for the night, but later woke to the sound of explosions. In the morning we learned we had stopped near an airfield which was bombed during the night.

We continued riding through small towns and rye fields, already harvested in a hurry, because the Russians did not want to leave the Germans a fresh supply of food. Those fields that could not be harvested were burned on Stalin's order, not to leave anything for the Germans who were quickly moving east.

By July 15, 1941, our convoy approached the town of Lubny. Night was closing in, so we stopped along the road for the night. We unhitched the horses, tied their feet so they wouldn't run away. It was my turn to guard the horses in the field while the others in the convoy fell asleep.

With pockets full of candies and a whip in my hand, I walked the field around the horses, when suddenly I was surrounded by a large group of people yell "Hurray." They ordered me to raise my hands and accusing me of being a German spy and flashing light signals to enemy planes. I denied it, and told them I had no flashlight. They searched me and found nothing. They told me that they were walking from Kiev to Harkov to report for military service. There was no other transportation.

Suddenly another wagon pull up behind ours and someone in the wagon used a flashlight. I called the attention of the group and they rushed to the wagon and began beating the people there. Many of them piled in the wagon and drove away to Lubny. I was saved, had I had a flashlight they would have killed me right there.

In the morning, we drove in to the town of Lubny, parked the wagons and reported to the military authorities for the men had to be cleared to proceed. Our director had all the papers and we were cleared; we even bought bread in a store reserved for mobilized personnel. We spent several days here in Lubny. There was a house where the great Jewish poet Sholom Aleichem lived in 1880 now a historic shrine, so we went to see that small house. In front of it was a big Russian sign about the history of that house and its occupant of long ago.

Again, the Director of the convoy had a conflict with Evelyn, me, and several other men. We left the Convoy and decided to proceed further by train.

July 18,1941, we boarded a freight train in the direction of Poltava. It was a flat car, and when I started to rain, we were soaking wet. Later the sun came out and we dried out, and managed to find room in a covered car where we spent the night, reaching Poltava in the morning.

About four kilometers from the railroad station at Poltava, our train stopped and the locomotive began wailing the sound of the siren. Other sirens followed. German planes were attacking. Our train held military supplies and was a target. A big German bomber came in low over the train, strafing it with bullets. People jumped from the cars and ran into the woods, Eveyln jumped off too but I remained aboard guarding our packages (silly!).

I lay on the floor of our car, but as bullets hit the car I got frightened and jumped out through the open door and into the ditch, along the tracks, just as the plane came over the car. I lay flat in the ditch for several minutes. Evelyn, looking out from the bush, thought I was dead.

When the sirens sounded the clear signal, we all returned to the train and shortly moved into the station.

Poltava had another railroad station on the other side of town, an evacuation center next to it which was our destination. We walked through the city, loaded with packages on our shoulders and in our hands. At the center we registered and waited for an assigned destination. Every day transports left from here taking people further east. Many were also sent to help at nearby collective farms.

Our aim was to get to the city of Harkov where we had an aunt, Hanna. When I found a train going in the direction of Harkov, we got aboard. The train carried a load from a dismantled factory, all kinds of machinery. It was very crowded but we were happy to be aboard. We were moving away from the war zone.

When the train stopped at a railroad junction named Merefy, some 30 kilometers from Harkov, we learned that the train would not go through Harkov but had been diverted in another direction. We tried to buy tickets for the local passenger train that was going to Harkov. But the Russian system was such that tickets were often not sold for so called lack of room. We decided to go without tickets. We managed to get aboard, but when the conductor later asked for our tickets, and we told him that we didn't have any, he led us to the police cabin board the train.

The officer fined us 20 rubles and told us that Harkov was under martial law and we couldn't go there without proper papers. When the train pulled in to the station in Harkov, the officer told us to follow him to the police station. We entered the police station and approached the commander at his desk and the policeman said that we came into the city without papers and that we paid the fine of 20 rubles.

The commander, upon learning that we were refugees, escaping the Germans began screaming at the policeman for taking money from us to pay the fine, and ordered him to also call in the conductor of the train. The policeman returned and said the train already left the station and the commander told us to come in the morning and get back the money. We were so relieved and went outside to wait for the morning.

Here, the little park at the station was again, full of people sitting on their baggage while waiting for a train, because no one was permitted to wait inside. We were lucky that it didn't rain, and the night was warm. We sat all night, occasionally one would sleep while the others watched the baggage and in the morning, I started out to find our aunt.

Chapter 17
Regina

In the ghetto Men were assigned to work details and issued identification cards by the governing body of the ghetto. No one could enter or leave without presenting an identification card. People without proper ID were presumed to be runaways and were taken away. My father and uncle got work cards. My mother didn't work, she was taking care of us kids. My youngest brother was only five at the time.

Much of the work we performed was so menial it was nearly pointless, such as cleaning mud from the tires of the German trucks. A German officer would inspect my job. One day he was not satisfied with my work and kicked me in the shin as punishment. This injury did not seem severe at first but would steadily cause me more and more pain over time.

To this day, I cannot understand how some people were so heartless. I know the Nazis indoctrinated the German citizens from a young age, instructing them to kill and torture small animals. By the time they were teens, many seemed to be unfeeling robots who would take any opportunity to punish other people.

One day the SS called everyone into the town square and said that all the rabbis and the members of the "intelligentsia" such as doctors and lawyers were to report to them. They were going to be sent to a different location in the countryside that was less crowded and dirty, we were told. They were complimented on their intelligence and told they would be put to work compiling an accurate list of everyone in the ghetto.

One rabbi's daughter jumped up and protested, calling them liars and questioning whether anyone would see their loved ones again after they were sent away. They shot her down on the spot and proceeded with the relocation process. A week after the trucks took the people away, their spouses who were still in the ghetto received letters inviting them and their children to join them.

But when all these people arrived in the countryside, what they found waiting for them there was a single mass grave. The SS shot them all, men, women and children. We learned this from survivors who had escaped. Killing off the intelligentsia served a psychological purpose because the Nazis believed that removing the brains of a community would make the remaining people less inclined to rebel.

In the Spring of 1941, around Passover we started seeing trucks arriving in the ghetto and noticed a lot of commotion going on. People were rounded up, pushed into trucks, and taken away. This also occurred again in late 1941 and became a regular event. The people who were taken away were never seen again. Each time one of these roundups took place, the ghetto grew smaller. The people who remained could only go on working and foraging for food as best they could.

We appointed sentries to watch the gate and alert the people when the SS was coming. I served as a sentry at one point. Similar events were taking place at other ghettos around Poland. We had an idea of what was going on in the other ghettos from brave people who escaped and spread news. Every roundup occurred at a major holiday. The next roundup was in September at Rosh Hashana, our New Year's holiday.

Chapter 18
Stanley

It was early on the morning of July 26, 1941, that I rode the streetcar to the center city square, and from there went on foot to the street where my aunt Hanna lived. People were suspicious of strangers but because my fluency in Russian as so good, I mingled with the crowd and after a few directions from people, found the house. The old lady who answered the door ran inside to tell my aunt that her nephew from the Polish side was here. Hanna was happy to meet me, but worried why the rest of our family wasn't with me.

Hanna lived with her son Liova, age 13, in two small rooms in an apartment building where each floor had a collective kitchen in the center and also collective bathroom facilities. All apartments used the collective kitchen and bathroom because no apartment had one of its own. Her husband left her when Livoa was born, because she called in a Moel, to circumcise the baby when the husband was not at home. He was a communist and did not believe in religion.

She worked in a factory and supported herself and the boy while her husband stayed away. He was sent by Stalin to a labor camp in 1936 and began writing letters to her to help him get out, but she did not want to hear of it and remained alone. She was happy to hear that at least Evelyn and I were here, but because it was time for her to get to work, we walked over to her sisters' son's house, just down the street.

Our cousin, Reuben was at work and his wife came with me to bring Evelyn and our packages. We were now among family and felt so relieved. But to remain in Harkov, we had to register with the police. Reuben helped with that and then we looked for jobs.

Throughout the city there were always long lines of people in front of stores, and because we were not working, we helped out the family by lining up for supplies I later found work in a lumber yard, unloading lumber from the freight cars, but soon the situation worsened. Supplies dwindled, and the German planes attacked daily. People marched daily to dig trenches and fortifications outside of the city and rumors circulated that soon we would have to evacuate.

By the end of August 1941, it was clear that we'd have to move on, farther east, if we were to survive. There was food rationing and panic. Hanna would not move, but our decision was firm to leave the city. Hanna and our cousin, Rueben worked and were not eligible to leave without an authorization. Evelyn and I registered in the evacuating office and moved our packages to the evacuation center in school #13.

This was a four-story building and filled with thousands of people in the classroom, or who sat on their belongings in the hallways. When there was an air raid, people stumbled over each other. Occasionally we met people from Kostopol.

Every day, larger groups of Harkov residents marched toward the outskirts of the city with their shovels and picks to dig trenches and build fortifications against the oncoming German army. The front was moving closer to the city and transports regularly evacuated people. At first I did not get a clearing to evacuate, because they wanted me to join the crowd for building fortifications but after some manipulations, we were assigned a transport to go to go to the German region of the River Volga, near the city of Saratov.

September 7, 1941, was to be our departure day and after standing in line for several hours with hundreds of people waiting to board the train, we found a compartment and settled for the long ride. With us in the compartment were two sisters and a brother from Kostopol who I had known at home. Another couple were also seated in our compartment, and we became friendly. They were Jewish, spoke a little Yiddish. Here name was Mania, his name, I have forgotten.

We settled into our seats and waited patiently for the departure, knowing full well that at any time there could be an air raid and our lives could be in danger. Toward evening, as the city lay engulfed in darkness, the train began to move to our destination, Engels on the Volga.

Our train moved fast, but soon began stopping for long

hours as we encountered military transports rushing to the front lines. The military had priority. Late that night I developed a toothache, and Mania, was up all night to help me. She was a pharmacist, and she had some medicines which she gave me and the toothache stopped. By morning we were already close friends.

Manie was a very pretty young woman of 26, attractive and friendly. Somehow, even in the closed confines of our compartment, we managed to have intimate talks. She confided in me about her personal life, and soon I realized she was in love with me, even with her husband around. She told me he was epileptic, and she did not want children. While we traveled in the dark, we found a way to be near each other, although I had no interest in getting involved in a love affair. But she was everywhere I went. When I jumped off the train to get hot water and did not come back quickly, she was right there looking for me. During the 10 days that we travelled together, confined to our compartment, we became so close that when we had to part, it was painful and Mania cried a lot. I never saw her again.

When our train reached the city of Saratow, the area where the Russian Germans had their concentrated towns and collective farms, we learned that the officials changed their minds and would not settle the people from this transport in the area, perhaps because most of us were Jewish, and the region was German, or maybe, something else. The fact was, that we had to move on.

Along the way, we encountered transports of German residents of the region, who were ordered to pack their belongings in two hours and be on the train—destination Siberia!

We passed railroad stations with German names, indicating that this was the German Autonomous Region, then crossed over the Volga and headed toward the Ural Mountains. Here on the others side of the Volga was no blackout, and for the first time in a few months, there was light at night and for the moment it seemed, there was no war.

Chapter 19
Regina

My family thought we couldn't stay there like sitting ducks, so we decided to find a way to hide. Some people made hiding places in the floors of their attic or the walls of their closets. My father and my uncle decided to build a bunker. We made sure it was invisible and not accessible to everyone. So, we turned the space in the basement under the stove into a bunker and built a false wall around it. We entered the bunker by lifting the metal plate beneath the stove and crawling in.

It took us maybe three months to construct this hiding place, but we saw how effective it was when the SS conducted another roundup. At that time a young couple appeared at our door and pleaded to let them hide with us. We denied having a bunker and tried to turn them away, but they threatened to inform the SS that we were hiding there, so we let them in. Everyone was packed in like sardines and nobody allowed themselves to breath. We gave a sleeping potion to my younger brother, who was about six and my cousin, who was two. We had to knock them out so they wouldn't cry and alert anyone to our presence. The SS came down into the basement and banged their rifle butts against the walls to see if anyone was hiding behind them, but the false wall held strong. It also helped that we were packed so tightly against the wall that no echo was heard. And so, we escaped discovery. Everyone breathed a sigh of relief. There were two more roundups after that, but the bunker saved us every time.

The monotonous hardships went on for over a year until the Spring of 1943. There was a knock at the door and my mother rose to see who was there, but my uncle stopped her and answered the door himself. He found himself face to face with a German soldier. He looked at my uncle, smiled, and shot him in the head with a pistol. My family was shocked to see our uncle lying on the floor with his brains shot out. That experience put tremendous fear into us. As much fear as we had before, this really brought it home that we weren't safe anytime, anywhere.

Then one day my father went to work and didn't came

back. Though we never learned his exact fate, we knew we were never going to see him again.

One night while hiding in our bunker, literally made stones we would gather and bring home little bits a time so as not to raise attention, Charna, a cousin of ours, had a three-year-old baby with her. She was so afraid that the baby would cry and give us all away that she decided to poison herself and her baby. She said, "I'd rather die with him now than let the Germans kill him with cruelty, at least this way we will be together."

I still can't manage to understand how she could to that!

Chapter 20
Stanley

Our train was stopped at the city of Uralsk, where part of the transport was directed to a small town named Chingirlau, the other portion to another region. Here we parted with Mania and her husband, and Eveyln and I and the two sisters and brother, (the Murautchiks) were brought to Chingarlau.

At the station we were met by officials who placed us in a wagon drawn by oxen. We were brought for the night to a local school. In the morning, we couldn't open the doors because a sandstorm had piled up sand against the doors.

Here in Chingirlau, the Murautchiks left for a collective farm, Evelyn and I remained in town. We took residence in a home with a Russian family and Evelyn found work in an office. I had no work but was out looking to find some.

Chingirlau, was a small town, surrounded by vast stretches of dry prairie (Steppe) where trees were scarce and winds always blew. It was already autumn and the cold winds made it worse. The fuel for the house where we lived was dry thorn bushes, which I helped gather along with dry sticks or straw. Water was taken from the Illetak River, which flows through town. The water in the river is very salty and had to be left standing for a while till the salt settled, then boiled to get the salt out. There was no other source of water, and like others I carried water in two pails hooked to a bar across my shoulders several times a day. It was quite a distance, perhaps a quarter of a mile. I was the only man in the house. The owner of the house was an older Russian lady whose husband was dead, and her daughter and child lived with her while the son-in-law was at the front. Another girl who worked in town and lived with us. There was no activity in town and the only source of information and entertainment was on a radio speaker connected to a main receiver that controlled all speakers in town.

After spending a month in this town, it became clear to us that we must move to a warmer climate. It became very cold; and we were not prepared for it, we had no warm clothing and there was no work. The place to go to was Tashkent, a city in Uzbek Republic where there is no winter and it's always warm.

We have already learned something about Russian geography and knew that the Uzbek Republic was far from the war zone and life there would be promising.

I had a piece of textile from home that I sold for 250 rubles, and with that little bit of money, we decided to start our move to Tashkent. After obtaining the necessary papers, we left town on foot, carrying our belongings on our back and in our hands.

The station was about three kilometers from town, and we walked in the rain and wind on the sticky clay road, reaching the railroad station wet and exhausted. Here we bought tickets to Buchara, in the Uzbek Republic and waited for our train, which came the next day.

This train took us to a central station, where we had to change to another train to take us to Asia and the Uzbek Republic. This station, Sol-illetuk and was an important junction on the railroad going to Asia. But here we faced a problem, which only people who travelled in Russia during the war would understand.

Tthe station at Sol Illetzk in the Urals was an important crossroads on the approach to the Asiatic part of Russia, especially the southern part where the climate was warm. Most important, there was security, being far from the front lines. All transports with refugees from the European part of Russia passed through here and all supply trains and wounded also passed through.

The station was not big enough to accommodate the thousands who flocked here, so people were not permitted to stay inside, but had to remain outside, around the station and in the small park near it. It was the end of October and cold, and our clothes were not suitable for that weather, so we shivered and hoped to soon catch a train south. We were hungry, there was no food available to buy, but to the credit of the authorities' hot soup was provided free and it was very welcome, even though we had to stay in line a long time in order to get it.

I was on constant look out for a train going in the direction of Uzbekistan and after a couple of days I discovered a train that was going to Tashkent, our destination. The train was parked on a side track, and we lost no time in boarding.

Because this train was filled with people running away from Moskow, who were not willing to give us a seat inside, we decided to stay on the outside of the car, and hope that when the train began to move, eventually the people inside would have mercy and make room for us.

The passengers of the transport were listed, and we were outsiders, and had we been discovered by the trainman, we could have been removed. We nervously waited for the train to begin moving and when it started we knew that it would be unlikely that we would be removed, for it was wilderness and the station were about 50 to 100 miles apart. We knew that we would make it to Tashkent.

We stayed on the platform outside the car and were happy that no one bothered us. But at night it was cold and we had to take turns to get in the car and warm up. To our surprise, in the morning, some people in the car became friendly and made room for us inside. They even saw to it that we received two loaves of bread and with some onions and radishes that I bought at some station; we survived the trip.

We traveled for five days through the dry steppes of Kazakhstan where you see nothing but sky and earth. Water was also a problem, because we had to stand in line for it and sometimes there was no time, because the train did not halt for long.

On the sixth day we were approaching Uzbekistan. it was as if a new world was being revealed to us! The sun was shining and it was warm. There were fertile fields and lots of fruit trees. There was no trace of war here, except for the military trains passing by.

On the outskirts of Tashkent, the capital of the Uzbek Republic, we learned that our train would bypass the city and in order to get to the railroad station, we had to get out and go by streetcar to reach the Tashkent station. From here we were to take a train to Buchara where there was already a great concentration of refugees.

Tashkent is a big city, perhaps the biggest in the Russian Central Asia area, and it made a very good impression on us. We were able to buy good food, particularly fruit, such that we had never eaten before. Some dried cantaloupes tasted very good. While waiting long hours at the railroad station we saw for the first-time people who were sick with malaria. We boarded a train to Buchara and within 24 hours we reached the central railroad junction at the station of Kagan where we got off. Here was a center for refugees where people were dispatched to different areas for settlement. Again, we stayed outside of the station, sleeping with our bundles among the thousands of refugees, each waiting to be directed to a permanent place.

Chapter 21
Regina

In the middle of June 1943, there were notices posted that the ghetto was going to be liquidated, completely purged of people. When the SS came to round up everyone, my family hid in our bunker for two whole days. Then my mother snuck out in the middle of the night to see if it was safe.

She returned and told us, "I think we are the only people still alive here."

Emerging from our hiding place, it appeared she was right. The entire ghetto was silent and deserted as a cemetery. We had escaped transportation to a concentration camp, and the near-certain death that awaited so many others there.

At that point we knew we had to leave the ghetto, but we needed someplace safe in the surrounding area to gather and hide. My mother approached someone my family knew from before the war and who my parents had been kind to. Her name was Mrs. Mukofski. My mother made her way to her house and asked if we could hide in the barn. Mrs. Mukofski agreed to help us and together we devised a plan.

Next to the ghetto was a convent with a tall wall. My mother instructed my two brothers to sneak through the grounds of the convent and out of the town to reach the Mukofski house. The rest of us would follow them one by one.

But in the process of scaling the wall around the convent, my brother Johnny fell and twisted his ankle. This attracted the attention of the nuns, who heard him moaning and came to help him. The nuns were very kind and tended to his ankle all night, but they said they could not allow him and Jack to remain there because the SS routinely checked the convent to see if the nuns were harboring any Jews. "God be with you," they told my brothers, and sent them on their way.

The nuns were so anxious about the boys being there but they couldn't turn their backs and when the germans came the next day to check they played it straight and said nothing.

Because the Germans were so meticulous with their record keeping they knew that my mother and her 4 kids were missing and they were determined to find them. The nuns were very brave to cover for us and we will be forever thankful to them.

Fortunately, they were able to sneak through the town and reach the Mukofski barn. Mrs. Mukofski received them very nicely.

The following night my brother Paul left, and he too arrived safely at the barn. On the third night, it was my turn. I couldn't jump over the convent wall, especially with my injured leg, so I had to disguise myself and make my way through the streets. I was afraid someone would recognize me but somehow, I made it. My brothers and I waited there for our mother. My aunt and nephew were also expected to join us.

While we were waiting, Mrs. Mukofski noticed the worsening condition of my leg injury where the Nazi officer had kicked me. The wound was now infected, and we feared my leg would need to be amputated. Mrs. Mukofski saved me from this fate by pressing a layer of cucumber skin to the wound. She applied a fresh layer of cucumber each day, and thanks to this treatment my condition greatly improved.

After three or four days, Mrs. Mukofski said she could not allow us to stay there because if she kept going back and forth to the barn her neighbors would become suspicious. She said we should hide in her wheat field and told us how to find it by counting the number of oak trees along the way and looking for a tree that had a picture of the Madonna on it. We followed her directions and gathered there in the field, staying low to the ground. The heat that day was merciless, and we were all wearing our coats because we didn't know how long we would have to be outside.

Our mother was supposed to meet us in the field but when evening came, she still had not appeared. Little Jack, who was only six, began to despair and started to cry. I did my best to comfort him and told him mommy always came through like she said she would.

The next day we were still hiding there. That afternoon Johnny stood up to look around and we suddenly heard a sharp whistling sound above our heads.

"What was that?" I asked.

"A bullet," Johnny answered, remarkably unfazed.

He was right. The German soldiers patrolling in the area knew that Jews were hiding in the fields, but it was impractical to search through the tall wheat to find them. So, to flush the people out they periodically fired their rifles at random to see if they could scare anyone into running. But we held onto our courage and stayed right where we were, and no one saw us.

Finally, at daybreak mother arrived. We were overjoyed to see her, but we noticed that our aunt and her three-year-old son were not with her. We asked where they were, but our mother said she would tell us later. Later when my brothers were asleep, I asked again why my aunt and nephew were. My mother told me that my aunt thought their chances of survival were worse than ours because her son could not speak Polish, only Yiddish. She had witnessed so much cruelty that she could no longer bear the possibility of having her son torn away from her and killed as she had already seen happen. The SS though nothing of killing a baby simply because it was crying too much. To escape such cruelty, my aunt had poisoned her son and herself. She was a very brave lady.

Chapter 22
Stanley

After several days, we were directed to the town of Gishdovan, some 30 kilometers away which we reached by an old bus toward the evening of November 16,1941. The bus stopped at the town hall where we got off and the night watchman sent us to a Uzbek Hotel for the night.

This was not really a hotel, but a Uzbek tea house, but it also served as a meeting place and if you needed a place to stay for the night. The tea house consisted of a large room, with platforms on both sides, some 2.5 feet off the ground and an aisle down the middle. Here people sat on the platforms, feet folded beneath them and drank tea from a tea pot that was placed in front of them. There were some Uzbeks who got for themselves a tea pot and kept drinking for long hours. Tea is their national drink.

Because of the influx of refugees, the tea house had begun serving as a sort of hotel, people sitting on platforms all night and occasionally drinking tea.

The atmosphere that night was tense as we heard that the Germans had reached the outskirts of Moskow and Stalin's speech to the Russian's was that soon they would be driven back. We hardly slept, taking turns watching our packages against thieves, a common problem, and made it to the morning. For breakfast we bought grapes and bread and with tea made a good meal.

Later in the morning, a young girl came in for tea and we learned that she was from the Ukraine, a town not far from Kostopol. Evelyn went with that girl to a farm where she lived while I remained at the tea house with our belongings. At the farm, she found several people from our town, who were happy there and who advised us to go to a collective farm. Our decision was made to do just that, and after obtaining the proper papers in the town hall, we set out on foot to the collective farm.

After walking for about 30 minutes on the narrow dirt road between the cotton fields, carrying our packages on our backs and in our hands, we reached our destination. The first to meet us was a young Uzbek who spoke a little Russian, and who introduced us to the Director of the farm. He welcomed us and assigned us a room. The room contained only a bed, broken windows, and when we got some bread, things started to look good. We were the first Europeans in their midst and they accepted us cheerfully. The next day a young Jewish boy from Poland was brought in and now we were three refugees. In the meantime, an old Uzbek began teaching me the Uzbek language, pointing to parts of his body with words in Uzbek. This was the most peculiar lesson I ever had in my life but I learned a few words.

Soon the boy and I were sent to pick cotton, while Evelyn remained at home.

Sunday, we walked to town to the market, bought supplies and it looked like we were settled in for a while. But one day a family of 18 was brought into the collective and we were informed that because their limit on Europeans was 18, and in order not to break up a family, we were to leave this collective and move on to another one, some kilometers away. Once more, we packed our belongings and made our way to the new collective, named Proletar. It was a bit smaller, and also here, we were the first Europeans. The first to greet us was the bookkeeper, a Uzbek who spoke a little Russian. They cleaned a storage room for us, bringing in beds, a stove and other things. When I asked one of the Uzbeks where was a window, he punched a hole in the wall and passed me piece of glass and there was the window!

The door opened to the outside and was often open in order to get fresh air. We chopped a tree for firewood and used it in the little iron stove. The warehouse manager brought in bread, raisins, and tea, and soon our room was filled with young and old Uzbeks, who came in to see the Europeans and learn something about the world. Again, we were content, but the next day new arrivals came.

The three Jewish families from the Ukraine were brought to this collective. Because their rooms were not yet read; they were temporarily put in our room. We became friendly and when they moved to their rooms adjoining ours, we entertained each other. I also started to work picking cotton and doing other farm work. Evelyn worked in the office, and I did other work. We started to learn the Uzbek language in order to communicate with the natives, who spoke a little Russian. Although the next town was only 5 kilometers away, many of the collective never have been there. They practice their native customs, among others the witch doctor who cursed illness by performing strange rituals.

There were no bathing facilities and so in the winter of 1942, the government ordered the collectives to build a bathhouse. We emptied one of the storage rooms, put in a big iron kettle without a cover on top of a small brick platform that we built, and under we lit a fire, which in turn, heated the water in the kettle, turning it to steam. This we called the steam bath and since the Uzbeks didn't believe in using a bath, we the Europeans were the only users. The process of washing was not simple, but we had to go on with it to stay clean.

Chapter 23
Regina

After two days in that field, Mrs. Mukofski said we were too close to town and that we should hide in another field they owned. So, we moved again and resettled in a new field. My little brothers could not sit still and would run around the field exploring. At one point they returned and told us they had met other people there. It turned out that we were not the only Jews that Mrs. Mukofski was allowing to hide there. There were six of them, including a distant cousin of ours. We united with them and embraced each other. It was a great comfort to have other people to share our burden with.

Together we tried to decide what to do next. We had two men among us and contemplated digging a bunker in the woods. After a few days there my mother was becoming nervous. She pointed out that the wheat in the surrounding fields was all straight and even, whereas our field now had a deep, visible impression in the crops from the eleven of us being there.

Sure enough, it was only a short time later that we were discovered by local peasants who were in league with the Germans. We heard voices approaching and moments later three men appeared and confronted us. We were frozen in place. We had lost the ability to talk and to think. Our captors ordered us to line up and march back to town. The shortest of the three men was at the head of the line, leading the way. The tallest was at the rear so he could watch over everyone. The third man, an older gentleman, was in the middle of the line, near me. In this formation we slowly made our way through the fields.

Suddenly Johnny bolted, disappearing into the wheat. The man at the back of the line shouted to alert the others, telling them to chase him down. Seeing my brother in danger, my ability to speak suddenly returned with a vengeance.

I turned to the man nearest me and barked, "So what, you'll have less blood on your hands?"

They stopped looking for Johnny and turned their attention

to me instead.

I went on, "Why are you going to bring us all in when we have silver, gold and other things that we can give you. What are you going to get from the Germans when you bring us to them? Nothing but a pat on the back for being a good collaborator. These are just kids. What did these kids ever do to you?"

The old man was looking at me with awe on his face. What I said had touched him, and his expression had changed. I don't know where I found such bravery. My brothers later said they wondered how I suddenly got such a big mouth. The three men consulted briefly with each other, then one of them said, "Okay, show us what you have."

I went around to each person in our group collecting anything of value they were carrying. My hands were full of whatever people had on them- jewelry, watches, even gold teeth. I offered it all to our captors. The three collaborators accepted this bargain, telling us, "Okay. We will take this and let you go, provided you don't tell the Germans we saw you."

I replied, "You better not tell the Germans you saw us!"

With that we were released from our captors and Johnny rejoined us. Everybody stood frozen in relief.

The other group of people still wanted to go to the forest and dig a bunker, but my mother decided it was better that we should part ways with them. She told them, "I'm going to take my kids and wherever God guides us is where we will go. I don't know where I will go or what I will do, but if God decides for us to survive, we will survive. But I'm not hiding with anyone else anymore."

So, our companions went on to the forest while the five of us hid in the fields until the harvest came and the fields were clean. This hindered our ability to hide. After that there were not many places to go. We sought out abandoned shacks and places with heavy brush and foliage. We dug up beets and potatoes to eat. At night we went to a creek to wash and fetch water. One day we hid on top of a haystack with our jackets spread above our heads to shield us from the sunlight. I thought that if we didn't die from heatstroke that day, God was truly protecting us. Thank God nightfall eventually came so we could climb down from the haystack and run to the creek. The cold water was a great relief after this ordeal.

Chapter 24
Stanley

During the winter of 1942 the situation on the battle fronts worsened and the Russians suffered defeats. The Germans were advancing up to the Volga and men were being mobilized if not to the army, then to work battalions.

One man from Kiev was called to work the Battalion and his wife, Hanna and daughter moved away from the collective farm nearby. They found a room in town and some work.

We came to visit them on Sundays when we walked to the market in town, an event that was important to everyone. Many of the farmers brought they products to the market, an open area in town sort of like a flea market; it was almost the only source of supplies for the people in the area. Here you had a chance to meet people, learn some news, get advice from others, and we even met one day people from our hometown. During one of these Sundays, when we visited our friend Hanna, we decided to leave the collective and moved to the town of Gishdoovan, temporarily finding shelter with Hanna.

It was one large room and we occupied one corner of it. We found work in a rope factory where we made ropes from cotton.

The process of making the ropes was simple. There was a board that had 4 hooks who were connected to a wheel and as the wheel turned so did the four hooks. Four people worked the hooks and one at the wheel. We wore an apron full of cotton and started with the cotton at the hook, twisting it while the hooks turned. Walking back, we made a string about 20 feet long, then combined the strings twisting them again until there was a heavy rope. But Evelyn couldn't continue the work with the cotton because of trouble with her eyes, so she found work in an office, while I remained at the rope factory. This was important because as a factory workers, I received 600 grams of bread daily while office workers only received 400 grams.

It was now summer 1942 and there were lots of fruits and vegetables around, but not too much bread. We were always hungry and short of money. Our financial situation was bad and when we received some news that our cousin Bluma and her mother and also Hershel were in Karshy, a city some 300 kilometers away, we decided to try our luck there.

We packed up a few package and I went out in town to find someone who would give us a ride to the train station, but when I returned to the house where Evelyn was, there were two Uzbeks waiting for me. They came to ask Evelyn to come back to the collective and to be the bookkeeper, because the bookkeeper was mobilized to the army.

They promised us good conditions which we could not refuse. So while we were already packed and ready to leave, we agreed to return to the collective and give it another try.

We were back in the collective Proletar, and this time they treated us with great respect. We were provided with a good room, supplies of food and things looked promising. Evelyn worked in the office and was paid with supplies, while I worked on different jobs in the collective and expected to be paid according to a day's work, when all the others in the collective were paid. This is the system on the Russian collective farms but while the others had reserves of food, we had none and that made a big difference. Superficially things looked good for us, but we were in trouble.

When we met our friends in town on Sundays at the market, we realized that our situation was not good. In the meantime, I got sick and couldn't work. I had continual pains and stomach cramps that I could hardly stand up straight. One day I walked to the clinic in town, 5 kilometers where they told me to get to a hospital for an operation on my appendix. I refused to go, but instead I asked the doctor for medication on a trial basis, perhaps to ease the pain. They gave me some powder, which I was to take with water and was told to return to the clinic in case it didn't help. I knew that I wouldn't be able to go back the 5 kilometers so I made it to the home of our friend Hanna and stayed the night there.

While I lay on the floor in the room, twisting from pain, the women in the yard thinking that I was asleep were talking about the way I looked, and that they didn't think I would make it through the night! I didn't want to die that night, my thoughts took me back to my home in Kostopol, my family, Evelyn in the collective. My temperature was high, and I only asked for tea, which Hanna gave me several times. I fell asleep ad when I woke up in the morning the pain was gone and I was like a new person! After having tea, I thanked Hanna for the hospitality and walked back to the collective again, five kilometers on foot.

In the next several weeks, I was mostly in and out of bed, couldn't work and lost a lot of weight. We were getting disgusted in the collective and meantime letters kept coming from our cousins in Karshy, urging us to come there. By late December 1942, we decided to go. The railroad station was in Kizil-tepo, a small town some 50 kilometers away. After making arrangements with the management of the collective and obtaining a release, we left the collective one evening, atop a wagon loaded with sacks of cotton which the collective had to deliver to the plant in Kizil-tepo for processing. After spending the night on the road we reached the railroad station by morning and again landed in a tea house and hotel, because the station was off limits. We had to wait till the next morning for a train, but tickets were not sold and we had to be alert for the train since they were never on time. We managed to get in the station for the next night and slept on the floor with our bundles, taking turns to watch for thieves.

When the train came in the morning, and even not having tickets, we managed to get in but were soon discovered by two conductors who forced us off the train, dumping our bundles outside. I resisted but lost the contest against the two. Because there was still time for departure, we grabbed our bundles and ran to the rear of the train and managed to get on board again. When the train began to move we knew this time we would make it, because there were no stations on the way where we could be taken off. We did have to buy tickets on board the train and also paid a fine, but toward late afternoon we reached Karshy and hoped soon to be with our cousins, whom we have not seen since the start of the war.

Chapter 25
Regina

At night my mother would sneak into the surrounding villages to visit people she knew from before the war to collect any food and supplies they were able to share. Our shoes were in tatters by this point, so people gave up burlap bags to wrap our feet in. But there wasn't much food for them to give us. Much of the local peasants' resources were being diverted for use by the occupying military. If you had two cows, one went to the soldiers. So, food was not abundant at the time.

As Winter set in and the snow began to fall, we adopted specific strategies to blend in with the environment and evade capture. In barns, we would huddle together in haystacks or lie close to the cows to stay warm. By this point we were wearing burlap on our feet instead of shoes and we would remove these rags and lay them atop the cows to dry. Jack would sleep huddled between my mother and I because he was smallest and needed the warmth.

When traveling on foot across the countryside, we used a large white bedsheet as camouflage in the snow-covered landscape. My mother and I would hold up the sheet to block ourselves from view while the others used tree branches to wipe away our tracks. In this way we would make our way across the fields without being detected. When we were hiding in unused barns or sheds, my mother did not allow us to plug holes in the walls to stay warm because people passing by might notice the repairs and deduced that the location was occupied.

At one farm, we hid in the pigsty because the noises of the pigs would help conceal our presence. This was important because I had developed a cold by that point and was beginning to cough. The pigsty was wet and filthy and smelled awful. But then a lady came to feed the pigs and she found us. My mother begged her not to tell anyone about us and promised that we would leave at nightfall. She also asked for hot water as well, to treat my cold.

The lady went away without uttering a word. Later she returned with a metal basin of hot water as well as cups and five white beats that she had cooked. White beats were often used as a sweetener because sugar had become a scarce commodity. We gratefully inhaled these supplies and the hot water combined with the sugar in the beats gave us instant energy and broke my fever.

There was another farmer who was very kind and allowed us to stay in his basement for three days. But then someone got wind that we were there, and we had to run away. We later learned that not long after we fled, the Germans came looking for us and searched the basement. The farmer tried to clean away any evidence that people had been living there, but the SS found a few eggshells in the basement. For that reason alone, they beat him so terribly that he later died of the injuries.

After that we found another place to hide at a farm where bees were kept. We stayed there for three days before the farmer found us. He was not a kind man and informed us with a stern voice that we were not welcome there, but my mother was able to convince him to let us stay.

She pleaded, "If you are a faithful man with God in your heart, leave us be and trust that we will be gone by daybreak."

"Alright," he agreed.

We moved on to an empty barn nearby and waited there while my mother went out in search of a better place to hide.

She met an elderly lady who arranged to meet with us later when she had food available to share. However, upon returning we were unexpectedly discovered by her son, who was not nearly as sympathetic to our plight. His mother urged him to have mercy on us, but he ignored her pleas. The son forced my mother in the barn and wedged the door shut so she could not escape. He left her trapped there and rushed off to alert the Germans. Her son was actually in collaboration with the SS and knew he would be rewarded for finding and turning in known fugitives.

During my mother's attempt to secure food at the farm, our family had become separated. She had brought Jack and Paul with her to the farm and left them to wait for her nearby. Meanwhile, Johnny and I waited at our previous hiding place. The purpose of travelling separately was to avoid attracting attention because five people together traveled more slowly and visibly.

The farmer's mother tried to let my mother out of the barn, but she could not open the heavy door by herself. My mother was so thin and emaciated that somehow, together the two women were able to open the barn door just enough for my mother to slip through and escape into the surrounding fields. My mother crawled along the ground for fear of being seen. She saw the trucks arrive to collect her. When it was found that she had escaped yet again, a furious search was launched. A group of Ukrainians was sent to look for us because many Ukrainians disliked the Poles and were collaborating with the Germans. These men cursed and punished the farmer's mother for letting my mother escape but thankfully they spared her life.

While my mother crawled through the fields, Johnny and I hid inside a haystack and Jack and Paul hid in a hayloft inside a tiny shack. Somehow, my mother was able to locate and unite us all. When we found Jack and Paul, we were amazed that Paul had climbed up into the hayloft in his emaciated state. He explained that he crawled onto Jack's back to reach their hiding place. We all shed tears of relief now that we were together again.

Later we heard that after this adventure, the town got together and asked the Village Elders "how could a woman with four small children escape all of the intense searching, between the soldiers and everyone in the village, after all we know everyone that lives here, how could she escape? Especially through the summer and the winter? It's just not possible!" We heard that this is how things were decided, the Village Elders decided to drain all the wells in the town, they claimed that it was impossible for anyone, let alone a small, woman with four children and no husband, to survive, so they thought that they will drain the wells, and in there they would certainly find all of their bodies, there was just no other explanation! They were convinced that she must have realized how hopeless their situation was and being at the end of the line, she must have drowned her children, and then thrown herself down after them!

But as it turned out, there were no bodies discovered. And now they all looked at each other with gasps of horror and confusion, how in the world could this be, it was the only explanation! Now the townsfolk started to suspect my mother was a witch. That was the only explanation they could come up with and the Village Elders had no ideas either. They just could not make sense of she and her four children could continue to evade the SS with all their patrols, trucks, and searchlights – for months!

Our life went on like that for nine months.

Chapter 26
Stanley

Karshy was a big town consisting of the railroad station and vicinity, and the town proper, which was about 7 kilometers from the station.

It was the county seat and served a large area of many collectives. There were several schools here and good industry and the chances of finding a job were good. Our hopes were great as we disembarked from the train, took our packages to the small park at the station (it was forbidden to be inside), to see what to do next. Since everybody was walking to town, Evelyn walked also to find our cousins, while I remained with the packages.

When toward evening Evelyn was still not back, I dragged the packages to the nearest tea house and watched the outside for Evelyn's return.

Later in the evening, Evelyn and our cousins, Bluma & Hershel showed up and when I saw them, I realized that we were in serious difficulties.

Their looks, their shabby clothes indicated to me that they were suffering, and were very hungry. We immediately began walking back to town, but managed to get a ride in a truck and were soon in town. The walk through the narrow dark (dizan) streets seemed endless and finally we made it! We opened a large wooden door that led to a yard and in the dark found the door to our cousin's room. It was dark inside and upon entering, I heard a voice coming from a corner that you could barely hear. It was the voice of our cousin's mother-in-law, Pearl, who was lying in bed.

When I touched her, I shuddered, as she was skin and bones and remembering her from home in Kostopol, I knew she was on the brink of starvation. We gave her raisins and bread which she quickly consumed, but also Bluma and Hershel were hungry and grabbed everything in sight.

In the morning, we saw their misery. The room was almost empty and shreds of cotton all over the dirt floor. Pearl could not get out of be, because of malnutrition. They had no money, no food, and did not work. They used up their ration card coupons at the beginning of the month and were hungry the rest of the time. I was ready to return to the collective, but Evelyn insisted that we stay. Meantime, Evelyn found work in a school as a bookkeeper while I looked for work in industry, to get a larger ration of bread. After scolding our cousins for not working, Hershel found work in a bakery and brought home bread every day.

Things started to look good, but then our situation became worse. We stayed with our cousins and lent them money and shared our food, but the supplies that we brought with us were now depleted and our money was being used up fast. I still looked for a job and I found after a few weeks an apprentice job in a plant that made equipment for horses. It didn't matter to me what the job was, as long as it allow 600 grams of bread, which combined with Evelyn's 400 grams, gave us one kilogram daily, things began to look up, again.

For several weeks our cousins were happy. Hershel brough home bread every day and Pearl got to feel better. But then, he lost his job in the bakery and in the meantime, Hershel was offered a job to teach in a school far away from Karshy. Because they were facing troubles again, Hershel accepted the job and they soon departed, leaving the room to us alone. The rent was minimal, and we were content. We had the feeling though, that we'dl never see Pearl again.

As our cousins departed we were able to clean the room and settle in. It was the beginning of the summer of 1943 and we realized that we had adjusted to the environment and made many friends. Evely was offered a job in a school, distributing bread for the employees, which she was to pick up in a special store, this in addition to her bookkeeping was a great help. I helped her out so in fact, we were both in charge. This was an opportunity to have lots of bread and do some business.

So besides my regular job during the day, we both spent evenings waiting for the bread to arrive, and then bring the bread to school to be distributed early in the morning before I left for work. It was hard work, but we did it regardless of the hours that were involved. One night that summer, as we slept in our courtyard, because of the heat inside the room, Hershel and Bluma walked in and told us that they all were sick with Typhoid and that their mother Pearl had died. They were hungry, their heads were shaved, their clothes were shabby. We gave them food to eat and the next day they registered for work constructing a dam near Tashkent. A few days later, they left town again, but soon, Evelyn came down with Typhoid and we were in trouble.

The epidemic of typhoid was all over. Evelyn was taken to the hospital and our room and all our clothes had to be fumigated, and because I wasn't home when it was done, there was a big problem getting everything back. But my biggest worry was no to get sick, so I could carry on with the distribution of the bread and keep my regular job. I kept on going from job to job, waiting every evening for the bread, getting up early to distribute the bread and then off to my regular job. There was no telephone to call Evelyn in the hospital and it was 5 kilometers out of town. There was no transportation and I had to walk 10 kilometers to see Evellyn and only speak to her from outside. Nobody was allowed to get close to patients. When I saw Evelyn for the first time, I got scared. Her head was shaved and she had lost weight. She spent one month in the hospital, and I visited there every Sunday.

Chater 27
Regina

We lived like animals outside, sleeping wherever we could, literally in fields in old barns, behind a wall or under a tree. I can still remember how hard the ground felt under us, and we slept in whatever we were wearing all day and all night. Through it all we just carried on, never asking why is this happening, we just did what we had to do and followed our mother's lead. Sometimes I was so scared to close my eyes I waited until sleep would take over. Then, exhausted from the day, we'd sleep as long as we could. I really don't know how my mother didn't lose her mind. My youngest brother Jack, probably 6 or 7 years old, was small and scared. at night my mother would put him between us.

"Why does he have to sleep between us?" I asked her. "I'm tired and I'm sick of this."

"He's young and he's having a hard time," Mother explained. "If he sleeps between us he will have the warmth of both of our bodies to protect him."

We had left the ghetto with whatever we could wear. In the summer, wearing heavy clothes was so hot, we thought we'd die of the heat, but when it started to snow, at least we had enough to help keep us warm, as well as some remnants of shoes. They were in shambles, barely a sole left. Our coats were ragged and full of holes. We were emaciated, skin and bones walking sticks of people.

The whole time we just went along with what Mommy said. We were kids. We had no idea why these people wanted to kill us, but we knew we were in danger all the time. We started to feel like caged animals, always looking over our shoulders, always on the alert, and always afraid. If we saw headlights from a car at night, terror took over. We'd be found and then what?!

We hid in abandoned homes. Many people left the village as the Germans took over and basically threw everyone out of their homes, burned them down and took whatever they wanted. There was no respect for people's homes, Jews or not, so hiding places were not easy to find, especially for four kids and my mother. That was a big group. We hid in barns, fields, behind stone walls, everywhere and anywhere we could be safe, whatever that meant.

We were exhausted. You could never really sleep and feel safe, so we'd just follow Mommy's lead and trusted her. The hunger was unbearable at times. We were skin and bones and anything to eat was absolutely amazing

One night Mommy told us to hide in the field of a friendly farmer. She took broken pieces of dishes and laid them in the rows as a marker so she would know where to find us. After a few hours she didn't return, we started to get worried and Jack started to cry. Then it started to rain. We got scared. She will never find us, we thought, so we left two of us together and went to hide somewhere else. We went to Stone Street, called that because each house had a large flat stone wedged on an angle indicating who lived in that house. We each hid behind a stone, crouching down and sitting quietly for what seemed like days, but was just an hour or two. At night no one was out walking around, there were no streetlights. Finally we heard a voice calling softly. "Jack, Paul, Regina, Johnny." One by one we peeked up to see our mother carefully looking for us. She said she knew once she didn't see us in the field that she'd have to think about where we might go. We all had learned how to hide. Meeting up with her was pure relief. Mommy was here, she'd make it right, and figure out what to do.

As much as I think I understood what was happening, looking back, I really can't comprehend it. I was just thirteen. All I knew was Mommy was there to lead and protect. We followed her and trusted her. She was FEARLESS, and impressive!

We lived outside for nine months, and she never let us get stupid. She'd talk to us about holidays, days of the week, made us count numbers, count lice on our heads, trees, whatever she could do to keep us thinking. She would talk about how things would be in case we survived, and always gave us hope that we would.

I didn't realize how lucky we were to have her as our mother. Another person would have cracked under the constant uncertainty, But she was tough! Always looking ahead and keeping us engaged in thoughts of the future, thoughts of how to braid a challah, how to count, history, holidays, and more. She was the original strong woman! I tell my daughter and granddaughter, "You come from a long line of strong women."

One night I was very sick and emaciated. A farmer brought a basin filled with warm water and beets that they cooked; they were like sugar. Tthe taste was heavenly and gave us such strength to go on for a few days. We needed that sugar rush, I wish we could have taken that liquid with us.

Chapter 28
Stanley

The month that Eveyln was sick was probably the hardest for me during the three and a half years in the Uzbek Republic. I held on to two jobs, from early morning to late in the evening. Above all, was my luck that I did not contract typhoid, which was unusual. I seemed to have good resistance and managed to escape it. When Evelyn came out of the hospital, I saw to it that she would eat well, and because it was summer and the best fruit was plentiful, it did not take long before she regained her strength. Our financial situation was good, and we could afford to buy good food. On the job, I was now the manager of the department with a lot of leather at my disposal. I had learned to make a special kind of slip-on shoe and sell it at the bazar on Sundays. I took the leather from my department illegally, risking a long jail term. I gave the leathers to someone who made the uppers and I attached the shoes at home. On Sundays the shoes were sold at the market, not by me, but someone else.

To get the supply of leather out from my workplace was not a problem, since I had good connections with the guards at the gate and in the central warehouse. Above all the director and his aide took some bribes from me. Many times, Evelyn came over to me during lunch hour and ate with me in our cafeteria, since it was reasonable and had available food. After lunch I manage to throw down pieces of leather on the outside of the wall where Evelyn would wait. She would pick it up and take it home and it turned into shoes which were bought for about 200 rubles.

We now had saved up money but had no place to keep it. We couldn't put it in a bank because it was black market money, and we had no connection to buy gold or other valuables. Our apartment had a dirt floor so I dug a hole in the corner, put the money in a round tin can, and covered it with dirt. Over it we stood a broom, and the money was safe. Occasionally we took out old notes and changed them for new ones. We were happy.

One day at the cafeteria, we met two sisters from Kostopol.

We were very glad to stumble upon people from home, especially younger ones. Lusia was a friend of mine since we were youngsters. The older sister, Sarah, I didn't know well. We had so much in common, being so far from home and always thinking of our families whom we left behind. Because we distributed bread, the girls came often to us and redeemed their rationing coupons, especially Lusia. Then walked her home. She was an attractive girl, and it was time now to enjoy life a bit.

Slowly it began to develop into a relationship which we enjoyed. The weather was warm and dry and we spent many evenings outside in the park or at the movies. The evenings in the summertime were hot, and we could take a plunge in the canal behind our house or in the small lake at the house where Lusia lived. I liked Lusia, we seemed to be in love, but we did not have plans yet, we just had a good time. I also made it clear to Lusia that until Evelyn got married, we'd just have to wait.

In the meantime, Evelyn gave up the distribution of bread, doing only the bookkeeping and I devoted more time to making slippers, which sold immediately. We bought supplies for the winter of 1943: flour, raisins, oil, dried fruit, and more. But on January 4, 1944, we were burglarized and everything that we had was stolen, including our clothes. Two days later our rationing coupons somehow disappeared, leaving us without bread for almost the entire month. Our savings dwindled quickly because we had to replace everything on the open market and things were not cheap.

In order to get back in shape financially, I dared to pull more leather from the plant, risking long jail time, if caught. It did not take long before we had the money back that we spent and even more. But the apartment was no longer safe, and we looked for another one.

In the summer of 1944, we decided to change our apartment and hoped perhaps that our luck would change.

I knew a girl who was making up the uppers for the slippers. She lived with her parents, a sister, and brothers. Her father was a tailor and they had a sewing machine on which she made the uppers for me. The girl's name was Tonia and I came there almost every week to give her work. At this time, we met a couple who came from Poland who also were looking for an apartment and when Tonia mentioned that there was an apartment not far from theirs, we got in touch with the couple, and together rented that apartment. It consisted of three rooms a small one which we subleased to a single man also from Poland, Evelyn and I in the larger room, and one smaller room for the other couple.

We were all Jews and had a common goal: to survive the war and return home to perhaps find our families alive. The war was not going in favor of the Russians and it seemed that the end was near. We had many friends and were in good shape financially and it was time to enjoy life a little. During the summer of 1944, I spent a lot of my time with Lusia. After all we were about the same age, from the same town, and we had known each other since childhood. Lusia attractive, and we had fun. But I was now living near Tonia, whom I saw very often, and many times in the evening Eveyln and I would come into her house just to spend time with her family. Slowly a closer relationship developed between me and Tonia, who was also my age. Shet told me about her past, that she had a boyfriend somewhere on the battlefield but didn't know anything about him. According to her, she was engaged to him in the Ukraine just before the war broke out, but I didn't believe the story because she showed a lot of interest in me. I was very welcomed in her house and felt comfortable there. There were always people in that house and we made many friends.

But at the same time, I also saw Lusia and liked her too. Here I was caught in a dilemma and Evelyn tried to maneuver me so that I wouldn't commit myself to either one. In short, I liked to spend time with Lusia but never thought of marriage and she knew that, but I also liked Tonia, but did not think seriously about her. I made it clear to Evelyn that I would not get married before her, and the girls understood that.

I was not really in love with Tonia, although I spent a lot of time there, sometimes in the company of her and a couple of her girlfriends who came to her house. But Lusia came often to us on the pretext that she wanted to see Evelyn and of course I was there and would escort her home. At times I was in love with Lusia, other times it was a slightly cool love.

During the summer of 1944, Lusia and Sara found their sister Fania, who they lost along the way somewhere at a railroad station in 1941. She was imprisoned in a labor camp, because she did not have her passport with her, and now she was finally released. Fania came to her sisters in Karshy and because she was a good seamstress, she got a lot of work, much of it for some important people in town. Eveyln and I came often to their houses and again, I was spending time with Lusia.

By now the Russian armies were pushing the Germans back much faster and we knew that Kostopol was already liberated. It was time to find out about our families. We sent a letter home but the letter was returned, saying there was no one at that address. We sent another letter to the town of Stepan, where my oldest sister Bracha used to live. This brought a reply from a cousin of ours, a young boy, who wrote that the Germans killed everybody and there were only a few survivors. It soon became clear that perhaps we had lost everyone in the family. The newspapers were writing about the German atrocities. We wanted to go back home but we also needed an affidavit from Kostopol that we were needed there.

We sent a letter to the town hall, requesting such a paper, and asked to list my name and Evelyn's. When the affidavit arrived shortly, there were three empty lines besides my and Evelyn's names; we filled in those lines with the names of Lusia, Sarah and Fania. We were now ready to prepare for the trip back home, but Evelyn and I first had to obtain permission to leave our jobs. Evelyn had no trouble reassigning her job, but I had a lot of trouble.

Because I was the manager of a department and responsible for inventory, namely leather, the director asked me first to take inventory, which proved a shortage of leather of a large quantity and my director demanded that I buy back on the open market leather replacement. It was a stupid demand and I told him that I would not do it, because the leather was stolen by workers, and it was not possible. He told me that he would not allow me to leave. When I replied that I would leave anyway, he said I would be arrested.

"If I'm arrested so will you be arrested because of the bribe that he and his Vice Director took from me." After several weeks of arguing, the shortage was declared a result of poor production and I was given permission to leave for home. Now preparations began and we started to pack and buy supplies for the two-week journey, and soon we were ready.

Chapter 29
Regina

In the ghetto, you could leave but you couldn't come back unless you had your ID card.

Early on in our escape, I had a problem with my leg. I had been hit on the leg by a guard and it never healed properly. Now I had a sore from a cut that turned into a bad, infected area. One night, it was so bad that I said to my mother, "My leg hurts so bad I can't walk."

Mommy looked at it and it was filled with infection and very red. I guess it didn't help that we had been sleeping on the ground. The cut was filled with dirt.

Mommy went to Mrs. Mukofski and asked for help. Mrs. Mukofski gave her a cucumber peel and some cloth. She told her to go to the river, wash the wound out to get the dirt out, and then put the cucumber peel on the wound and wrap it with the cloth, and to keep doing that. The first time mommy took off the cloth my leg looked completely brown! But she kept on the cucumber peel and cloth wrap and within a week the sore was healed and I could walk again!

Years later, in the U.S., at a doctor's visit the doctor asked me what the scar was from on my leg, I told him the story. He started at me in disbelief and asked me over and over again, how did she do that again? Cucumber peel? WOW!

Now I say to my daughter, if I ever complain about anything, slap me! I've been through so much, there is nothing to complain about!

***

The changing of the seasons only increased the monotony and misery of our existence. I have no idea how my mother stayed strong and positive; she never gave up, always looking at our next move, thinking about where we were going next, always planning always thinking.

Paul grew thinner and thinner, and it became harder and harder for him to walk. He was quiet, always listened to Mommy and now he was getting quieter and now I can say probably depressed. Johnny, always a bit on the wild side, became increasingly impatient. He wanted to join up with the Polish resistance to fight the Nazis. That was his personality, the tough guy, always ready for a fight, always ready for an adventure.

I stayed steady, following Mommy's orders. I was the oldest, the only girl and I knew she relied on me to keep the boys in line and to keep things in order. There was no room for girly thoughts, no thoughts of things like regular pre-teen/teenagers would think of no thoughts about clothes, no thoughts of simple things like brushing your hair, or friends. There were the five of us and Mommy was the leader. I too was thin and emaciated, dreaming of the day when we could have a normal life, and I could brush my hair, take a bath, and wear beautiful clothes. But those were dreams. In the present it was hide, survive, watch my brothers, listen to Mommy, and try to make it one more day. The future, well it wasn't even clear if there was going to be a future. We lived minute-to-minute and happy to wake up the next day, all of us still together.

Six-year-old Jack had no toys, barely any food, and he was so thin and cold at night! I could see the age on everyone's faces, but I said nothing, I didn't want to add to my mother's burden by pointing out the obvious.

Despite all of this, my mother held us together. I was continually amazed by her persistence, ingenuity, and ability to improvise in the face of extreme danger and hardship.

And she knew how to talk to people! Somehow, she was always able to convince people who were strangers to us, to assist in any way possible, even though we were known fugitives. I was always in awe, and thankful that she could connect with kind, brave people who would share their meagre provisions and not betray us to the Nazis. Maybe they saw something in her that reflected their own kindness and bravery – if the tables were turned how would they feel and how would we act toward them?

This was especially remarkable because the SS had used the original roster of people in the ghetto to determine what individuals were unaccounted for. That's how they knew we were missing.

During our travels, the peasants we spoke to informed us that the SS was on the lookout for a Jewish lady with four kids who had somehow eluded capture and was presumed were hiding in the area. My mother assured them that with their help, God would continue to keep us safe. And they went about their business and did not report us. They were simple, poor people who had no idea why this war had come to the area, but I could tell from the way they spoke to my mother and looked at us, that they understood, at a deep level, and they passed along information to us, and let us go on.

My mother demonstrated the persistence of someone who had blinders on. All that she was focused on was the wellbeing of her children. She was determined to survive! While in hiding she even took the time to tutor my little brothers in their math skills by having them count the number of lice they killed. She made us remember and recite the days and holidays, anything to keep our minds focused and sharp. She never let our present misery distract her from the hope that our family would go on with our lives and prosper.

Part 3
Liberation and Peace

Chapter 30
Regina

We had no idea what was going on in the outside world, we had no cell phones, no one to talk to and so we just kept moving as best we could trying to survive.

Paul, the second oldest was so weak, he was emaciated and could barely walk. The night before what would be liberation, he told us all, "just leave me here, save yourselves. I'm a burden, you can't carry me anymore and I can't walk! Go on and leave me." He said what we were all thinking but would never say, and as kids, we didn't know any better. When you live like an animal you start to think like an animal and just focus on yourself, survival and where your next spot of food or water would come from.

But mom would not hear of it! She gathered us all together and firmly said, 'we came this far, no one is leaving anyone behind. We are in this together and we will survive and carry each other if we have to take turn."

When I think about her, the total bravery and her absolute determination to save her family, I'm speechless! I admire her so much for never giving up!

The next day we found a barn to hide in and we were so thankful for a place out of the cold. When we got inside, Jack got down on all fours and we boosted Paul up to the loft; he could barely get himself up but we pulled together and did it.

Then we all climbed up to the rafter and saw there was a hole in the roof. We talked about patching the hole with straw to keep out the cold and wind. "No, the farmer knows his roof has a hole in it," Mommy said. "If he comes and sees straw sticking up he will get suspicious and we don't want to draw attention to ourselves."

We waited and tried to warm up. then when daybreak came we were woken to a chicken squawking because it had laid an egg, right in front of our eyes! The chicken's squawking attracted the attention of the farmer! The fear that went through us was indescribable. We finally had a place to stay that was warm, out of the weather and we could rest, and then this! I thought to myself, stupid chicken, SHUT UP, I just want to be here for a bit without anyone finding us, why are you making such a big deal!

When the farmer appeared, we were frozen in fear. My mother immediately went to work. She begged him not to say anything to anyone about our being there. "We will leave immediately please, just please bring me some hot water and food, we will eat anything we just need some food, please!". The farmer merely turned and walked away.

Again, we found ourselves frozen with fear. I could see my mother starting to gather and plan to leave, right away. Her words echoed in my mind. "We've come this far, we are staying together no matter what." I could see another endless day of trudging around ahead of us, surely the farmer was going to turn us in. But miraculously the farmer proved to be a kind, gentle man!

He returned with the hot water, some food, and said he would allow us to stay in his barn, My mother immediately thanked him for his kindness and offered him blessings; he said nothing. This made her think that while he's being kind, we couldn't be sure of anything so she assured him that we would soon be moving on as promised.

"You're not going anywhere," he told us. I literally froze in place! He is going to capture us and torture us, or burn down the barn, or who knows what! Why would he say that? I could see my mother's concern in her eyes, as her fear grew and grew, she yelled and pleaded "Please, please, don't report us, please!"

But the farmer, calm and steady, shook his head and pointed his finger off toward the horizon.

"Listen," he told her.

Now we were all confused, what were we listening for? Had the farmer lost his mind? But in the distance, we could hear booming, like thunder. We had no idea what that was, but the farmer seemed calm and continued to speak to us in a kind way.

"The Russians are coming," he said

I wasn't sure if that was good or not, and the other kids didn't have a clue either! I waited anxiously to see Mommy's reaction.

She was surprised, and I thought that was a good sign. She

was not panicking or looking at us anxiously. Iit seemed like this might be good news.

For months we had been so focused on day-to-day survival that we lost track of how the war was progressing. The farmer told as that after much bitter fighting on the Eastern front, the Russians had counterattacked and gained the upper hand against the Germans.

Chapter 31
Stanley

One June 11, 1945, we, together with the three Tabachnick sisters, Evelyn and I left town and moved to the railroad station, which was 7 kilometers away. Here again we had to stay outside in the little park next to the station where all the passengers stayed. Staying inside was not permitted and because it was summer and no rain there was no problem. We bought tickets only to Kiev, in the Ukraine because the cashier could not find the price of tickets to Kostopol. We waited two days until the train arrived. When the train came and we went to our assigned car, the girl in charge of the car would not let us in, stating that there were no empty seats. I objected to her refusal to unlock the door but because the train only remained here for 15 minutes, there was no time to argue. I motioned the girl that she'd get 200 rubles if she let us in immediately. She unlocked the door, and we got on board with our 10 suitcases. We found our assigned seats empty of course. and made ourselves comfortable and the train began to move. We were on our way home!

A short time later, the girl in charge of our car came into our section and winked at me to follow her. As we entered her cabin, she wanted from me the 200 rubbles. I told her that I would like to transfer our group to the car that would be attached to the Moskow train when we came to Tashkent, and I'd pay for it. We knew that one car from our train would be hitched to the Moskow train, and the passengers of that car would not have to wait in Tashkent for weeks to get a place on the train. The girl came later with the head trainman and told me that for 1,500 rubles they would transfer us to that car. But when I checked later, I found that the car in question was not destined for Moskow but rather was full of wounded soldiers on their way to a hospital. Learning that they wanted to defraud me I refused to pay. I offered the girl 100 rubles, but she refused so I gave her nothing. She then sent a controller to our car, and he confiscated our tickets, claiming that our suitcases were overweight and above the limit. I later threatened the girl that I would call the police and finally the tickets were returned to us. The girl received nothing from me.

After 24 hours on board, we reached Tashkent, where we had lived four years before. This was a big city, a major junction on the railroad in Central Asia. Like all passengers, we had to settle in at the park near the station for a long wait. There were thousands of people sitting on their luggage, afraid to sleep because of theft. The police were helpless and urged people not to sleep, so we alternated, someone always on guard. One day we met a girl from our town who told us there were a few boys from Kostopol living in Tashkent. Lusia and I went to see them and at the same time, saw the city had grown enormously during the war. It was now filled with tens of thousands of refugees from the European part of Russia. The city transportation system consisted of street cads, but there were many donkeys in the streets and I saw a street car pushing a donkey, who not get off the tracks.

We were lucky and spent only three days in Tashkent before succeeding in transferring our tickets from the Moskow train. In order to get aboard, there were long lines, so I found a porter who was willing to smuggle us to the train through a back door. It worked and when the train was loaded, we were among the first aboard and settled comfortably in our compartment for the long trip of five days to Moskow. As the train began to move north, making its way through the prairie and desert of Asia, we passed small villages and isolated railroad stations, several big towns, but mostly vast empty land. We realized just how big Russia was. At some stops there was bread for sale, most often though there was nothing. At one station I bought a pail of salt which I traded later for 500 kilometers of bread. At the Lake of Aral, we bought dried fish, which we brought with us to Moskow.

At the end of five days, we were nearing Moskow, and the scars of the war became more visible. The landscape changed rapidly and there were now many towns close to one another, quite a contrast from the Asiatic part of the country. We were back in Europe and close to home, but what kind of home it would be we didn't know, or most important, who had survived.

Our train pulled into the Kursk Station in Moskow, but to

continue, we had to get to the Kiev Station, a long distance away. It was a rainy morning and we had to follow our baggage on foot through the streets of Moskow until we reached the Kiev station. Here the authorities s permitted us to stay inside the station, so again we settled for the long wait to transfer our tickets to another train to Kiev. In the meantime, we needed bread, which was not available. After learning that as passengers we were entitled to buy bread in a special store on the other end of the city, we took a ride by subway to that store. This was the first time that we rode in a subway and what a trip it was!

The Russians call their subway the Metro, and it was very nice. The Metro was built in the early 1930s, it was modern and especially clean. The Russians thought of it as a show case, emphasizing Russian progress. The white tiled stations were clean, the stores were nice but hardly anything was available to buy. There was no pushing and shoving aboard the train, the people were polite. We saw Red Square and the Kremlin and after obtaining the bread that we were entitled to, we returned to our place at the Kiev Station.

After three days of waiting, we managed to stamp our tickets again, going through the ritual of pushing until we got onboard the train to Kiev. Here it was not crowded and comfortable. There was hardly any room to sit, never mind a chance to sleep. We saw the scars of the war: burned out stations, skeletons of burned trains, a memory of great battles at the approaches to Moscow. When the train stopped in Briansk, an important junction on the railroad, we were told that it would remain here for one hour. I got off the train and ran to the nearby little marketplace, a usual shopping place in Russia, to buy more bread.

But as I was about to buy a loaf of bread, I heard the whistle and saw our train jolt. Abandoning the bread, I jumped over tracks and around freight cars, running as our train slowly began to move. Luckily, I jumped onto the steps of our car and managed to get inside. Had I not made it, without my passport and money, which Evelyn kept, I would have been arrested and it would have taken a very long time to establish my identity and be freed. It wasn't very long before we arrived in Kiev, the capital of the Ukraine.

When we got off the train, and looked around the scars of the war were visible everywhere, and already rebuilding had begun. The last time we were here was July 1941 in the midst of the war, when the air raids were going on all the time. At that time, we were running away, not knowing where to go and what we would find, now we were going home, but not knowing what we would find there. Our letters home were not answered and we were prepared for the worst.

Chapter 32
Regina

Cannon fire could be heard continually in the distance for the next several days. And that meant there might be an end to this nightmare. We stayed in the barn, and the farmer was very kind and helpful. We were so relieved to have a place to stay, but our consistent fear and lack of trust, for even a kind farmer who shared good news with us made it impossible to really rest.

One day, we didn't hear cannon fire, and wondered what it could mean. From our secure hiding place we began to hear voices speaking Russian. My mother knew Russian and we had started to learn it in school but I didn't know much or what any of it meant.

Of course my mother remained suspicious and forbade us from revealing ourselves to the Soviet soldiers until we could be sure it was safe. But after so many days of being cooped up in the barn, Johnny got restless and suddenly we noticed that he was missing. Again, my mother's words 'we've come this far, we stick together" rang in my mind and we all realized Johnny, being who he was, had disobeyed our mother and ventured off to greet the Russians on his own.

We had no idea what to do. One of us had left the pack and after all these months of sticking together through everything, the idea that one of us wasn't in the group was impossible to handle. I could see the fear and worry on my mother's face as thought carefully. Should she go after him? Or stay with the others? Russian soldiers coming was good news, they could save us, But…her boy out there on his own!

An hour can be an eternity when you are worried and waiting. Finally, Johnny came back. When he returned, he was confident of course. That's just how Johnny was, right out in front, tough and bold and nothing was going to get in his way, I admired that confidence in him.

"The Russian soldiers met me on the road and at first they were skeptical when I said my family had hidden from the Germans for so long."

They told him that they had been marching since Kiev and not encountered a single Jewish person.

"They asked me where rest of the family was, but I refused to tell them where we were hiding," he boasted proudly. "I told them that my mother would kill me if I told them!"

Then the village officials tried to force him to talk, and they questioned him over and over about where the rest of the family was hiding and wanted to know his name and how he and the family could have survived. No one believed him but he stayed steady and repeated the story over and over. Finally, the Russians interceded and gave Johnny a sack of biscuits and let him go.

When Johnny returned, we could not believe that he brought food. And that he was safe. We cried. My mother yelled at him, then cried, then thanked God for his return, and then we ate!

He told us all about his adventure and in true Johnny form, he was big and bold and boasted of how he stood up for us and never told anyone where we were hiding. The feeling that the family was back together was overwhelming and we all settled in for a nap and a night of togetherness.

The next morning, my mother felt it was safe to leave our hiding place. After Johnny's story, the kind farmer, no more cannon blasts and a good night sleep, she felt it was time to walk out to meet the Russians.

At first, she was skeptical, keeping all of us behind her, but after general greetings and niceties, the Russians gestured to her that it was ok and like a scared, beaten animal she slowly approached, careful to keep a few steps ready to retreat if things went badly.

The people were kind and wanted to help. They were amazed that my mother had kept four children alive in the frozen, war-ridden countryside.

"Where do you come from?" they asked incredulously. She explained the insanity of the last nine months and told of our hiding, starving, sickness, and how we finally arrived here by the miracle of God.

The Russian soldiers, in awe, said they had been marching

for six days, all the way from Kiev, and have not encountering one single living Jewish person, let alone children. Their eyes were wide with astonishment and admiration. They saw our looks of exhaustion, fear, and of things no one can even explain, and their eyes met ours with kindness and understanding.

"By the grace of GOD and good people, we are here, and we are alive," my mother said.

The soldiers were kind and helped us recover from our ordeal at the hands of the Nazis. They washed us, cleaned us, and shaved our heads to rid us of lice. They advised us to eat slowly as to not upset our stomachs. They gave us blankets and beds, finally we could rest!

Paul, who was next in line after me, was also the tallest and skinniest of all, especially for his height and age. He was so emaciated he could barely walk. At the trepidation of my mother, who vowed to never leave any of us, she finally allowed the Soviets to transport him to a field hospital where he was nursed back to health after several days.

We sat in awe, homeless, beat up but still together. It took us days to even begin to relax and realize what we had been through, where we had been and where we were now. It seemed like a dream, well more like a nightmare, of what we survived, HOW we survived and now here we were, recovering from months of pure insanity.

The war in Europe officially ended on May 8th, 1945.

Chapter 33
Stanley

We had to wait a few days to get the train to Kostopol. Evelyn and I went to see our friend Hanna, who was already back in Kiev. Passing through the city we saw the devastation. Kiev changed hands several times during the war, each battle bringing more destruction. We saw baby-Yar at the Podol, where most of the Jews from Kiev were killed and buried in mass graves. The beautiful Kreshtatic Street was in shambles.

Returning to the railroad station, Lusia told us that she met a Jewish Russian officer who lived in Kostopol in1940-1941. He told her that he was just returning from there and thought that our house was still standing. At this news, our hopes to find someone increased. Soon we were again onboard the train, moving toward the old Polish border, now part of the Ukraine.

There was absolute destruction all over and remains of burned-out vehicles and equipment scattered around because there was not yet time to cleanup. The train was crowded with local people who were on and off the train often because of the closeness of the station.

Not far from Sarny, a town some 30 kilometers from Kostopol, three Jewish girls came aboard and into our compartment. They survived the war in the forest and they told horrible stories as to what happened to the Jews in the area. We got very friendly with them and caught up with them later in Rovno, on our way to Poland. Finally, we arrived in Sarny in the morning, but we had to wait there all day for the evening train that would take us home to Kostopol.

Sarny was a familiar town from before the war. I had friends my age who were members of our Zionist organization "Hashomer Hatzair." We met with them occasionally at conventions and they came to Kostopol to our local organization. I was in Sarny also for a convention in 1940, when we were already under the Russian rule. When we got out of the train, it was terrible to look at the devastation. The big station was gone, and rubble filled the nearby streets.

I asked a railroad employee if there were any Jews here. He told us that in one of the streets there was a house occupied by Jews. Evelyn and I went there and found a group of Jewish teenagers living in a commune. They told us that they were the survivors of many Jewish communities in the area and that most of the Jews were murdered. They also knew my cousin Lusar, who survived alone, and now was on his way to Poland. We returned to the station and toward evening took the train to Kostopol.

The car we were in was a freight car, now used as a passenger car and all around us were Ukrainians and some Russians. Evelyn, myself, and the three Tabatchnick sisters were the only Jews on that train. As I looked at the faces around us, I couldn't help but think that perhaps some of them were participants in the murders committed against our people, who looking at us, wondered why there were still Jews left.

After about one hour on board the train, the familiar landscape began to emerge. We passed the Iron Bridge, where only four short years before I walked so often with my friends as we roamed the forest on weekends. My heart pounded in anticipation of what we will see when we arrived.

Soon the train passed the crossing on the highway and houses were visible, the plywood factory, and we stopped at the railroad station. We have returned to my birthplace – Kostopol!

It was almost dark when our train pulled into the station and to our surprise, it seemed nothing had changed since the war started. The police officers seeing Jews advised us to remain inside the station for the night, explaining to us that there were bands of Ukrainian nationalists, called Benderas, who while fighting the Russians also killed many Jews who survived the war. We brought our packages inside the station and slept on the wooden benches inside;, we felt somewhat safe as the station was guarded by Russian police.

Leaning on the bench, with my eyes closed, I recalled events of five years ago, when my father and I were waiting here on these same benches long hours, for the train on our travels to Lvov, shopping for goods. Then, there were Jews all around us and now we are alone, 5 Jews returning home after a terrible war, uncertain what we would find and whether anyone of our families survived.

When morning came, and passengers began to arrive, I felt like crying, being the ONLY Jews at the Station. Everyone in sight was Ukrainian or Russian but no Jews.

Evelyn and Lucia went to town to scout and later returned in a buggy, owned by the only Jew in town, Max. Max was a fireman before the war, and he owned a small candy store. Now, he was in charge of supplies and a BIG WHEEL.

The Ukrainian driver helped us put our baggage into the wagon and we started moving. Riding through the street we could see most Jewish homes were boarded up, a sign that no one lived there. There was no destruction, just empty streets, and not one Jew in sight!

The wagon pulled up in front of the house of Aliosha, the salami maker, a neighbor of the Tabachnick sisters who was very happy to see us alive. We knew Aliosha from before the war and he knew my father well. He told us about the massacre of the Jews in Kostopol, including my family. We were now prepared for the worst and after leaving our packages in the temporary apartment which was assigned for us, together with the 3 Tabachnick sisters, in the home of Chechslovakian family on Copernika street, Evelyn and I went to see our street and see if anything was left or our big house and perhaps miraculously maybe some of our people survived.

We walked through the long highway street, where we so often walked for many years before the war, and met only a few people on the street, then turned into SKarbowa Street and soon, we were turning into Rovenska street where our big house stood.

Our hearts were pounding faster as we neared the place where the house once stood. There was no sign that there ever was a house there, only a potato field lay between the road and the orchard, in the back of our barns. Also, the couple of small houses which stood on both sides of ours were also gone. The rest of the houses on the street were in place, their Jewish owners – murdered. The new owners had been our Ukrainian neighbors of before the war. Many of them robbed Jewish properties and were perhaps accomplices in the murder of our people. Here in the street, as a child, I played with other Jewish children, often in mud puddles until the street was paved with cobblestone in 1934. Until then the water in the street after heavy rains was a great source of activities for us children. Later when paved, the street served also as a racetrack for our bikes.

Now, after four years of a terrible war, Evelyn and I were the ONLY survivors of a large family, a part of the small number of Kostopol Jews who survived the war.

We were stunned as we shed tears. It was unbelievable that of such a large family and Jewish surroundings, NOBODY was left. We stopped at one of the neighbors' houses and found a Ukrainian family living there. We recognized the woman of the house, whose family were our neighbors before the war. This woman used to do for us some housework, especially on the Sabbath, like lighting the fire in the stove during the winter, milking the cow, tending the garden and other work and knew us well. But she did not recognize us or did not want to. When we identified ourselves, the woman started to cry, telling us horrible stories.

She claimed that she often brought some food to my family at the Ghetto fence, a story that we really did not believe. After returning to the apartment on Copernike Street, brokenhearted, and after discussing the events of the war years with Aliosha and other gentiles, we got a good account of what happened here during the German occupation and the complete atrocities they committed against the Jewish community of Kostopol.

Upon entering Kostopol, June 29, 1941, the Germans shot several Jews and ordered restrictions for the Jewish population. Shortly after that they took out by force most Jewish young men for work in a labor camp. Soon all were killed. Among them were my two brothers-in-law, Mojshe and Shmuelik. Before they were murdered, the Germans made them write letters to their families, that they were ok and that they wanted the families to come and join them.

Later, the Germans proclaimed that in order to join their husbands, all families should assemble at the stadium and to bring belongings and valuables. When the women and children came on the appointed day to be reunited with their husbands, they were surrounded by German and Ukrainian police. They were ordered to take off their clothing, which was placed with the valuables on waiting trucks, and then they were led naked to nearby ditches, where they were shot on the spot and later burned. Among them were my two sisters and their children. The rest of the Jewish population was then moved to a Ghetto, in one street near the public bathhouse, where they lived, crowded and in inhumane conditions, many died of starvation and disease. Several hundred Jews were also placed in the two synagogues adjoining the Ghetto where apparently my father and the rest of the family were held.

The end of the Jewish community came in September 1942, when the last survivors of the once flourishing Jewish community of Kostopol, were taken to Hotinka, four kilometers from Kostopol, on the road to Rovno, where they were shot and buried in a mass grave, many buried alive. Among them were my father, my mother, and probably my sister Rivka.

In total, our immediate family losses were:
- Father – Mordechai
- Mother – Pearl Dina
- Sister – Braha
- Her husband – Mojshe
  - Their children
    - Fajgele (6 years old)
    - Nacuhm (11 months old)
- Sister Rivka
- Sister Hanna
- Her husband – Shmelic
  - Their daughter baby girl, born on the first day of the war (6.22.1941), name unknown

In addition, our family lost uncles, cousins, and many relatives who also lived in Kostopol and in neighboring towns. They are too numerous to list.

May their souls rest in peace - שתנוח נפשם בשלום (Hebrew spelling?)

I promised my parents on the 27 of June 1941 that I would return, and I kept that promise. We had returned, but to our extreme sorrow, found our family murdered, buried in mass graves, a part of our 6,000,000,000 martyrs.

Stanley and Evelyn,1947

Chapter 34
Regina

Our old house in the village where I grew up had burned down, so we stayed at my grandmother's house, which was located near a railroad depot. We were finally free, but life was still a struggle because we had very little to eat and no clothes. We were also afraid of influential locals who had sympathized with the Nazis. Although the war was over, there was ongoing tension between the Soviets and the many Ukrainian internationals who were around. It was a time of great disorder and mourning.

My mother wondered how we should move forward. What about everyone we knew from the village? Did they survive? Where were they? The worst part was, there was no time for mourning, or processing what happened, it was survival again, but this time at least we felt safer.

We remained at my grandmother's house until 1946, slowly gaining our strength back, finding our footing, and starting to find ways to live. It was a strange time, not sure who we could trust, and not speaking about all the experiences we had over the past nine months was strange, I felt like I wanted to talk about it, but at the same time, we were all happy to move on!

Again, I found myself at my pre-teen/teen years with nothing but duties to the family, my mother and grandmother. There was no school, no opportunities to hang out with friends, just daily chores, and we were happy to have them, but at the same time, and now in hindsight, the idea that we survived all this and then were just expected to go on with our lives is bizarre! We were never offered PTSD counseling or support, it was never even a thought, you just toughed it out, grateful to have survived and move on with your life.

Eventually, we made our way by train to a displaced persons camp in Fohrenwald, near Munich. GERMANY! I can't imagine how my mother felt about going to Germany, but I know I felt like the world was spinning upside down! Why would we go there, I thought?

My mother was instinctively afraid to go to Germany of course, but there were about twenty such camps organized by relief organizations, scattered about Germany. It seemed that was their way of making things right.

When we arrived it was interviews, paperwork, and the entire time, Mommy kept us all together, close at hand. When it came to us, the guard, unphased by all of us, just doing his job, barely looked up and yelled, "Name!"

She stated her name calmly and without emotion. "Clara Brottman."

"Where is your husband?"

She answered obediently and without emotion—by this time emotion was a foreign feeling, there was no room for it. "He was killed.'

"Do you have any children?"

My mother stood up a bit taller and stated calmly, 'Yes, I have four children"

This got the official to stop, put his pen down, raise his glasses to his eyes and look her in the eye like she was some kind of alien, he never seen before. I could feel my mother's grasp on my hand, fear started to run up from her feet to her hands and her eyes started looking around the room at the others, was everyone getting the look she got?

The man looked at her again and said, "I'm sorry, but did you say you have FOUR children?"

My mother stood tall and confidently, held us all even closer and said defiantly *"YES, I DID, IS THERE A PROBLEM?"* Months of hiding, fighting to survive, starving, and praying to survive had hardened her and now was NO time to be questioning the impossible that she and the four of us somehow managed to survive! She couldn't understand what the questioning was for. Had she done something wrong? Why was he staring at us?

Now he stood up, and said "PROBLEM, THERE IS NO PROBLEM! THERE ARE BARELY ANY JEWISH CHILDREN LEFT, HOW IN THE WORLD DID YOU SURVIVE WITH FOUR CHILDREN? HOW OLD ARE THEY? WHERE ARE THEY?"

The man continued to stare at us and said "I'm just

astounded that you are here, standing before me, alone and telling me that you survived with four children! Lady, I have no idea how you did it or what you did, but good for you, welcome!" He looked over my diminutive mother with awe and amazement. How in the world could this tiny woman survive with four children, and they are all alive?

She explained, calmly and with confidence, how we survived. Detailing our ordeal over the last 9 months and how she kept us all together, no matter what. She held us tight and showed the man that yes, here we are, see!

I think in that moment the shock and extreme focus of our survival and all the close calls, sickness and moments when she wanted to give up all came flooding back to her and it was a sudden moment of reflection, I'm sure she asked herself, 'HOW DID I DO THAT?' but as quickly as those thoughts came, they left and she was back in this giant room, being questioned and being processed, whatever that meant.

Chaya, left, with her children, Regina, Jack, Paul and Johnny

Chapter 35
Stanley

The only thing that remained in place of our big house was the small cherry tree which grew in front of our home and appealed to every passerby with its tasty cherries. It now stood as a monument to a large family, cut down by the murderous hands of Nazi Germany, people who committed the greatest act of genocide in the history of mankind.

We knew we could not settle here. Jewish life was now being threatened by the Ukrainian Nationalist Bands who were fighting the Russians, and they had no problem killing Jews. We were happy that our home for the moment was Kopernika Street, just opposite the military post in the home of Dr. Gasko. This gave us a sense of security but fear gripped us constantly.

Our apartment consisted of two rooms which we shared with the three Tabachnik sisters. When Jewish soldiers realized that opposite their post were Jewish residents, they often came in and spent some time with us. We felt more secure with them around. But when we walked the streets, the town was not the same. While there was no destruction here, the streets were almost empty, except on market day, Sunday, when the farmers and peasants brought their products to sell. The market area I remember from before the war with its two rows of stores and the nearby synagogues, was now a big lot, void of the synagogues and stores, but full of Ukrainians who wondered "how are there still Jews around?"

One day the mailman brought us a notice that there was a care package at the post office for the Jewish community of Kostopol, so we went there and claimed to be the Jewish community and received the package. We were shocked realizing that the five of us were now the entire Jewish community of some 8,000 Jews of pre-war Kostopol.

Another push to leave Kostopol, was also the fact that when I came to report to the police my presence, as is always the case in

Russian, the officer told me that they need Jews who are trustworthy, to accompany, with a machine gun, the wagons with supplies from the nearby villages. Knowing that many Jews were killed after liberation at the hands of the Ukrainian nationalists, I was not ready to risk my life and we began planning to go to Poland, where a mass concentration of Jews was going on. The Tabachnik sisters decided for a while to stay.

By now, several Kostopol Jews had returned from Russia and were directed to our apartment. They usually spent a few days here, but most soon left for Poland.

One day a truck pulled up in front of our house and four Russian soldiers came into our apartment. One told us that his wife was a Jewish girl from Kostopol, and I knew her. He asked whether we'll testify that the girl had a house here, which was still in place. I told him yes, and learning that they were going to Rovno, where we wanted to go to give up our Russian passports and take back the Polish passports. We asked them if they would take us along in the truck. They readily agreed and so we got on the back of the truck. Evelyn, me and Lucia, the four soldiers in the cabin and we were off.

But as we got out of town some four to five kilometers, the truck suddenly left the road and into the forest. At this moment, it appeared to us that the soldiers were Ukrainian nationalists, who knew we were Jews and would kill us now!

We could do nothing but wait. When the truck stopped in a clearing, the soldiers jumped out and apologized. They said that they are going to take logs on the truck and then would move on. I helped load the truck and then we got on top of the logs, riding safely to Rovno! We did arrive and we weren't killed. Here we began looking for Jews, and for temporary shelter.

We met a little Jewish girl in the marketplace, and she invited us to her house where her mother lay in bed sick, as a result of months in hiding from the Nazis. The woman let us stay in the house and gave us a place to sleep over, while we had to settle the problem with our passports. An agreement with Poland gave Russian citizens who were born in Poland a choice, to either remain in Russia or accept a Polish passport and go to Poland.

We chose to give up our Russian passports and go to Poland. We saw no point in remaining in Kostopol, where the ground was saturated with the blood of our family and our people. We felt like strangers in our homeland.

Evelyn and I went to the appropriate office, where at the same table sat a Russian officer and a Polish Officer. While giving up the Russian passport we immediately received a Polish one. We were also assigned a date for a transport to Poland. After a few days in Rovno, we returned to Kostopol and began preparing to go on to Poland.

Lucia and her sisters decided to remain in Kostopol. Evelyn and I were going to Poland. But even so my going away was painful. Lucia and I were somewhat close, and we were in a predicament, I wouldn't leave Evelyn and she wouldn't leave her sisters. She said that they would shortly also leave for Poland. And so once again, we took our few belongings and walked to the railroad station in order to leave the town where we were born, but also the place which was now soaked with the blood of most of our family. A light rain fell, and as we walked in the early morning toward the railroad station, our mood was somber and sad. We were leaving Kostopol for good, never to return to the place where the lives of the town's Jews, including our family, men, women and children, were cut short, by the hands of Nazis and the Ukrainian collaborators. Their bodies lay buried in mass graves, but we don't know where. No monuments to their lives, no tombstones, essentially no trace of them having been here, contributed to society or anything about them remaining.

As we walked, my lips uttered a curse, that the area now desolate of its Jewish inhabitants, the soil soaked with the blood of our people, should also consume those who participated in this annihilation of the Jewish people, and that the area should become, once again, as it was many, many years ago.

We arrived in Ruvno in rainy weather and had a hard time carrying our bundles a long distance to the house of the woman and her daughter whom we met before, and we found shelter for now. We found in this house, warmth and generosity and really felt comfortable on our short stay. All that remained now was to wait and check out, when our transport will assemble and we were now impatient to join the thousands of Jews who were streaming into Poland with the hope to make it to the Land of Israel.

The day of departure was a long one, for it took all day to load the 18 freight cars that were our transport. Nine of the cars were Jewish and the other nine were loaded with Poles who were being resettled to Poland. Because of that, the Poles carried with them their belongings, furniture and even domestic animals, and the Jews, many survivors of the Holocaust who managed to recover some of their tangible properties, and newly acquired belongings also had much to be loaded on. We only had a few packages and many others like us how have returned from Russia also had only very little of baggage.

For us, it was easy to get aboard and settle in. The others struggled throughout the day to get everything aboard and finally the next morning, we began to move.

Our train traveled in the direction of Lvov, a familiar I 'd traveled many times before the war. In those days, my destination was known to me, now we didn't know exactly where our destination was. There were rumors that we were going to Bitom, a German city which was now part of Poland, and where there was already a large concentration of Jews. Others thought we'd go to Lodz, a large city with many textile mills. But we knew that we were far away from our destination, and so we had to make ourselves comfortable and tried to enjoy the ride.

We got friendly with our neighbors in the car, made friends with people in other cars, forgetting for a while the problems we would face upon arriving. At the new Polish border, our train was checked by Russian border guards, and while we sat in fear, it all went well and we moved on.

We were now in the new Poland! The towns and villages we passed appeared poor and at each stop there was nothing to buy. As we were nearing Lublin, we saw in the distance the chimneys of the gas chambers in the concentration camp Maidanek, where millions were put to their death, most of them Jews. It was heartbreaking and sickening to think of it. Over the same tracks, just not long ago, millions traveled the last road before they were gassed and burned in crematoriums. Now, we were traveling the same route, free and eager to start and build a new life. But the haunting of that scene and the idea that all those had no idea what was going to happen to them, was just more than our minds could handle and while we looked forward to starting a new life, feelings of sadness, utter disbelief, and overwhelming guilt came over us.

Because I always liked to sing, I was able to entertain and that took our minds off everything and everyone in our car enjoyed themselves. There were always people coming into our car and we entertained each other, forgetting that we were traveling to an unknown destination and complete uncertainty.

When we reached Warsaw, the capital of Poland, our train was moved to a side track at the station and was parked. When evening came there was talk that the underground Polish national army, an illegal organization, sometimes attacked trains, especially when there were Jews on board, and it was decided that all Jewish men should be alert all night, and so we spent a sleepless night watching and waiting. The next day a rumor spread that our train would be sent to Prussia, a new territory that Poland received at the end of the war. The Jewish half of the transport had no desire to go to Prussia, so a delegation was sent to the Authorities, to intervene in the matter. We all contributed money to bribe officials, and that made it possible for the nine Jewish cars to be sent to Bitom.

The nine Jewish cars would be disconnected from the others and pushed quietly to a small station four miles away where a locomotive will take over. Around midnight, we quietly disconnected the cars and all the men began them and then jumped in while the cars rolled slowly to the small station and halted. A locomotive was provided and soon we were brought to a large station where we were transferred to passenger cars on the way to Bitom.

We were moving south, and this part of Poland looked in better shape. There were more stations, larger cities and we were able to buy supplies. The ride was more comfortable and within two days, we reached a station near Bitom where we disembarked. From here, we took a streetcar to Bitom, while all the baggage was brought in later to the market square and dropped off there. We wondered – where do we go now.

Bitom had been a German city, but it was in the area that Poland took over from Germany, while giving up some territory in the East which the Russians annexed for themselves. It was now a center for Jewish survivors who came from Russia, concentration camps, and hiding places in the forest, as well as partisans and demobilized soldiers, all who sought a way to get out of Poland. There were already organized Zionist activities, Kibutzim and an underground organization to move Jews out from Poland, on their way to the Land of Israel. There was a Jewish governing body, a special committee in the city of Katowice, nearby, which handled matters of the Jewish refugees who were coming in large numbers, every day.

Upon our arrival, we were surrounded by Jews wanting to help. Evelyn, I, and a few others from our transport found an abandoned building on the corner of the market square, which had no owners and without asking anyone, we just moved in. At last, we had a roof over us and we settled in until further exploration for permanent settlement could be made. We met several people from Kostopol who like us, came in from Russia and didn't know what to do next.

The building we found shelter in was a large apartment house, but the floor we were on was empty with only several rooms suitable for living, one of which we took over. The plumbing was not functioning, and doors could not be shut, but somehow, we remained there for a time. There was a kitchen but it could not be used since nothing in it worked. We did not prepare any meals but rather bought food as we were always out trying to buy and sell goods on the open market and at the same time discussing with others our options for the future. The transports with Jewish refugees from Russia kept coming, and on one of them, Lucia and her sister came. I went to the station and brought them to our apartment to stay with us for a while. Our apartment was now a kind of a commune. We slept on the floor and on beds, all in the same room, people came in and debates were going on regarding what to do.

A few times, I travelled with partners to other distant cities in occupied Germany where we brought with us food supplies and returned with goods which we sold on the open market. Travelling in those days was very dangerous, since the trains were always crowded, standing for long hours and always being on the alert, because the trains were not on time, many times people rode on the outside steps between the cars or on the roof outside the cars!

It was the way to make some money to get by. While traveling by train, I tried to mingle among Russian soldiers, speaking Russian and wearing a military shirt with a wide belt and flared out pants and boots. This was helpful when confronted by Polish personnel who were harassing Jews, suspecting them of some kind of black market business.

Here in Bitom, late in 1945, were many Jews, Kibutz, and Zionist clubs where the boys and girls met and spent good times in a Zionist environment in preparation to leave Poland and eventually reach the Land of Israel. I was among those young people and made friends and planned with them how to get out of Poland. Although I spent a lot of time with Lucia, which in reality was a love affair, I did not want to get tied down to her.

As the fall progressed, we saw no choice but to leave Poland. We had no ties, no income, no home. Evelyn and I decided to leave Bitom, while Lucia and her sisters staid. We registered with the organization "escape' which was funded by American Jewry, whose job was to help Jews to get out of Poland by any means.

The boys and girls who worked as guides in the organization often risked their lives as they led Jews over the borders, in order to come to the American Zone in Germany, or to Austria, where there were already UN camps for displaced persons.

In early November1945, we were ready to leave Poland. Our group consisted of about 200 people and according to our falsified papers, we were Greek Jews returning home from concentration camps. We were told to have little baggage, only a shoulder bag and perhaps a small package, and be dressed to look Greek. We were told if possible, to only speak Hebrew so it would appear to the Poles that it was Greek, and those who couldn't say anything in Hebrew, should be silent. Because I spoke Hebrew, I was one of the leaders of the group.

On departure day, we arrived at the railroad station in Katowice, and I approached two station employees at the exit gate and asked them in Hebrew what time the train was leaving for Bratislava in Czechoslovakia. The two Poles did not understand me and one said to the other "what the devil is he saying?" I understood them but pretended that I didn't, and kept repeating the same question in Hebrew. Finaly, they caught the name Bratislava and showed me on the watch that it was 8:00 o'clock. I then ordered the group, in Hebrew, to follow me, one, two, three, and we got on to the train. On the way to the Czechoslovakian border, there was a silence except for Hebrew songs that some of us sang.

It was late in the evening when we arrived at the border, and changed trains in the morning, to get to Czechoslovakia. As we began leaving our train, another train pulled into the station, filled with Russian soldiers. While passing a group of soldiers, standing in front of their train, one of them turned to me with a question – where we were going and before I had a chance to reply in Hebrew, a man walking near me replied to the solider with a prayer in Hebrew.

The Russian soldier immediately completed the prayer in Hebrew and said to us in Yiddish, that he was a Jew from Poland and that he would follow us some day to the Land of Israel. It was a tense, unreal, and emotional moment. Did this just happen I thought?

For a moment, we were concerned but all was all right and after waiting all night at this station, in the morning, we left for Bratislava and took up temporary shelter in a dilapidated hotel which was now being run by our organization, the Braicha Escape.

Here were hundreds of Jews, waiting a few days until arrangements were made to go on to Germany. To the authorities, we were Greek Jews, going home from concentration camps, and when one real Greek came to town having no place to go, the Police brought him over to us, but the boys at the entrance said that he was not Greek since he spoke Greek and they replied in Hebrew, thus convincing the police that he was not Greek, despite of his insistence that he was, and he was turned away.

After three days in the run-down shelter, we received

papers that we were German Jews, returning home from concentration camps and by train reached Praga, the capital of Czechoslovakia, where again, through assistance of the Braicha, were gathered in a shelter for a few days. Here we had a chance to tour the city and again by train, we left for the German border, accompanied by boys from Braicha. In Karlsbad we got off the train and walked to an abandoned Villa, which was a gathering place for the next trip. Which was by truck to the town of Ash on the German border. This was necessary to avoid military check-ins. That night was very cold, and in the villa there was no heat. We broke some furniture and put it into the fireplace to keep warm and in the morning, left.

Here we again gathered in a building and at midnight were instructed to follow a couple of guides across the German-Czech border. We walked silently through the forest in a single line, hold onto one another, in total darkness for eight kilometers, and by 6 a.m. we emerged from the forest to the railroad station where we took a train to Munich, the central pathway place for the remains of the Holocaust.

Munich, the central city of Bavaria, was the birthplace of the Nazi party in Germany, where Hitler organized the first riots in a beer hall of that city. Ironically, now those who were its target for extermination were gathering here to start a new life. The Deutches Museum teamed with thousands of Jews who came from Russia, Poland, Romania and other countries of central Europe, all waiting to be directed to a camp in the American zone in Germany, which was supported by the United Nations Relief Organization. We joined a small group and were directed to Camp Fohrenwald, which we reached by train. We were not permitted to enter through the gate, and with the help of people inside the camp from a kibutz, we entered the camp through a break in the fence and settled in the Kibutz quarters of Hashomer Hatzair.

As youngsters, Evelyn and I were members of Hashomer Hatzaiir and we were familiar with its aims, namely, to come to Palestine and help build the Jewish homeland. Now, it appeared to be the chance to realize our youthful dreams of going to the promised land.

Later we registered in the camp office and we became now

official residents of camp Fohernwald. Our long journey of some 10,000 kilometers, which started in Uzbekistan, Soviet Asia, and ended in Bavaria, Germany, where the Nazi party was born and who succeeded in annihilating 6,000,000,000 of our people. Here, in Germany, where the Jews were murdered, the survivors of this Holocaust gathered again temporarily to take shelter in the Displaced Persons Camp and awai the time to go to the Land of Israel, or other parts of the world, and begin a new life.

What an incredible, sad, frustrating, fear-filled, and horrible experience this was. Camp Fohrenwald was built for workers of the nearby arms industry, which among others also produced parts of the U-2 rockets, used to bomb Britain. The buildings were two story apartment complexes with streets, making it look like a small village. By the time Germany surrendered, the camp was vacant and when the US forces intercepted thousands of Jewish inmates which the Germans were still driving on a death march, they were freed and began being placed in camps such as Fohrenwald. Soon more Jewish refugees arrived from throughout central Europe, all survivors of the war and of the Holocaust.

The camp was governed by its own elected governing body, its own police (unarmed) and other administrative offices which any small town would normally have. It was under the jurisdiction of American military rule, and the German authorities were not permitted to enter. Around May 1945, the numbers in the camp grew quickly, and by the time of our arrival, there already 6,000 Jews there.

Evelyn and I were designated among the founding members of the Kibbutz of Hashomer Hatzair, and because of our knowledge of Hebrew, we were important. There was already a functioning Hebrew School of 300-400 children who lacked teachers and the search was on for anyone who could teach. Soon Evelyn and I were invited to teach at the school, and a new challenge in my life began.

Although I had the knowledge, I lacked teaching experience, but because of my activity as a leader before the war, I gained the new required experience rather fast. Taking some pointers from a couple of older teachers and putting my heart and soul into it, I soon became one of the best teachers in school and most beloved by my children. During the years 1947-1949, I was one of the triumphant of three teachers who were running the school. There was no principal.

Stanley with his students at Camp Fohrenwald, 1947

Chapter 36
Regina

Once we entered the camp, we could see the familiar look of war on the faces of the others. It was a blank, solid look, almost void of emotion, that's the only way to survive, no emotion allowed!

A doctor at the camp said Jack, who was very underweight and under where he should be in height, needed treatment for breathing problems. My mother was of course suspicious and very reluctant to be separated from any of her family. She insisted on seeing the sanitorium herself before letting her son be admitted. After she was satisfied that he would be safe and it was clean and he would be treated properly, she allowed them to bring him there, she saw many other displaced persons were being treated at the hospital. Frostbite was a common ailment among them. Jack spent most of 1946 in a nearby hospital run by the camp.

There really wasn't a lot to do in the camp, we were just happy to be safe and see others who looked like us, with that blank, lost look and a SMALL glimmer of hope for some level of normalcy.

Local people donated books for us to read. They were all in German, but we were happy to have anything.

I didn't know it at the time, but Stanley, my future husband, was also in the camp, after his own ordeal. He was only 22, and somehow was appointed to be a teacher for all the kids.

He would stay up and translate the books from German to Hebrew. He was more educated than most of us, and knew that we could all read Hebrew, so he translated as much as he could.

There was no formal classroom and no grades, we all went to school together, kids from six to sixteen, all lumped together and all eager to learn, be with other kids and have some sense of normalcy.

We were all happy to be distracted by something new and to learn and grow, instead of being on the run, not knowing our future and in survival mode all the time. In fact, all the kids that survived and learned in the displaced persons camp later when they got to the US, all excelled in US schools!

The kids in the camp were wild! After living like wild animals for months, somehow surviving absolute terror but not understanding why they were forced to hide, beg, steal, live in filth, be near starvation and not allowed to cry, they found themselves in a safe place with others who were just like them! They were alive and let themselves go and were wild!

Many had been living in the woods, lost parents, been separated from family, and seen things no one should see, at any age. They just wanted to be kids, to feel safe, loved, and cared for. Not only were they starved for food, they were starved for love. They had learned not to trust anyone, approach carefully, and always be ready to run and hide.

To them, Stanley was THE ONE! He was young, he was smart, he too was a survivor! He spoke their language; he was an adult (well almost) but he was one of them. He gave them attention, and for those starved for love and a connection to someone they could trust, he was everything. They clung to him not only as a teacher, but as a friend, father figure, counselor, advisor and guide.

Stanley taught history; he taught from donated books. Whatever the subject was, he pulled together lessons. They respected him, looked up to him and learned from him.

To organize the kids and try to control their wildness, he gave them structure, starting with a daily march around the camp. Every day he would get the kids together, have them stand in line from shortest to tallest, and then parade them around the camp. They loved this.

They walked proudly through the camp, with teachers who themselves were survivors, and as the days passed, regular people started to join the parade. Teachers would carry a flag and march around the camp for all to see. After a few days, adults would come out of their homes and wave, cry and yell with excitement *"we have children!"* Many of them were mourning the loss of their own, but thrilled that another generation would live on.

Chapter 37
Stanley

At the start, in 1945, it was very difficult and challenging. We had no textbooks and most of the youngsters, having survived the war, had never had an opportunity to attend school. There was a mix of older and young children in each class. Under normal conditions, this is not tolerable, but we struggled with it and somehow succeeded. By 1946, we were able to place children in classes where the age and knowledge were on the same level, thus creating a normal environment for education.

In the meantime, Evelyn met a man in the camp, and within a few weeks they were considering marriage. And it was to take place soon! In January 1946, Evelyn and Albert got married and moved into their own room, while I remained at the Kibbutz.

Early in January 1946, Lucia and her sisters came to Germany and settled in camp Freiman, some 35 kilometers from Fohrenwald. We soon met again, and our relationship resumed once again. We had some mutual friends, generally had a good time, and no particularly big worries. We knew that the DP camps were temporary, hoped that the UN would help solve the refugee problem and we will be able to resume a normal life. The more time I spent with Lucia, the more I was reluctant to consider our relationship serious. She was attractive and very appealing as a girl but I was not ready to talk about marriage. Since Evelyn was now married, my excuse that I would not marry before Evelyn was no longer valid. But while I loved Lucia to a certain degree, I wasn't sure that she should be my wife, so we just stalled for time. I was devoted to my work in school, and because of my affiliation with Hashomer Hatzair, I also recruited many youngers in school to join our organization.

I taught Hebrew, geography, Jewish history and above all singing and organizing plays. Not having textbooks, I often used old German geography books, even translating them from German into Hebrew. I also translated Russian songs, adapting Hebrew words which the children learned to sing, thus learning Hebrew rapidly. I was loved by the children, for I was not only their teacher, but after school I was their friend. The teachers were respected by the parents and the children.

In June of 1946, Lusia came to Fohrenwald where we both attended the wedding of a friend who was from our hometown Kostopol. By this time I was close to a decision to get married and discussed it with Lusia. At the wedding, Lusia talked with a boy who said he was going the next morning to Munich, and Lusia told him that she is gong also. She slept over in our Kibbutz room and in the morning left for Frieman.

A week later, her brother-in-law, David, came to Fohrenwald and told me that Lusia was getting married to the boy she met at the wedding! I was shocked, but relieved, because I knew that I was not genuinely in love with her. Soon I was informed that she was not getting married, but was leaving for Palestine through the illegal way which many Jews were using. She said that she would throw herself into the sea. I didn't even react. We met later once more at a friend's home in Frieman, at which time we spoke briefly, and I wished her all the best. I never saw Lusia again, but years later, while living in America, a boy from Kostopol, who just came from Israel, told me he saw her in Israel. She was married and divorced. In 1976, on our visit to Israel, I met Lusia for the first time in 30 years.

Regina and Stanley with friends at Camp Fohrenwald

Chapter 38
Regina

What is so astounding now, is that none of us had any kind of PTSD counseling or anything like that, it was, "Okay, you survived, you are alive! Now get on with it!" Harsh when I think about it now, but at the time that was the way it was and we had no reason to question it. In fact, we were happy to have survived. Shocked, terrified, and in complete disbelief that it all happened, but alive!

By this time, I was nearly 17 and really didn't understand why kids parading around was such a big deal. My mother kept us safe, and we had survived, purely by the grace of God, good people, and my mother's shrewd and unrelenting dedication to keeping us safe and surviving no matter what.

For entertainment and a project all the kids could focus on, Stanley and the other teachers organized plays. This was a great way to bring everyone together and channel their energy.

One of the plays was about the *'Charpoones'* a Russian word that was about the capture of young boys. The story was that the czar in Russia put a rule in place that any thirteen-year-old boy would be taken and put in the army, so parents started to hide their boys! The *"Charpoones"* were the capturers. Stanley created a play about this as a way to teach the history of *"Charpoones,"* and the kids loved being involved in something creative.

He put on other plays, coinciding with the Jewish holidays like *Purim*, as a way to remind everyone about what was important and keep them diverted to doing something creative.

The camp even organized trips for us to get some culture. We went to castles and other cultural places in Germany. Odd because this was also the country where people had tried to kill us! I remember coming to the U.S. and not wanting to buy any German products. Why would we support a country who tried to wipe all of us off the face of the earth!!!

Chapter 39
Stanley

In 1946, we finally made contact with our sister Lea (Lilian), who was living in New York with her family. We began making plans to go to America. I had to leave the Kibbutz, and I moved in with Eveyln and Albert. Although I was no longer a member of the Kibbutz, much of my spare time was spent there because of the many friends that I had.

Late in 1946, I met a girl who was visiting relatives in the Kibbutz, and between us developed a relationship that was followed up with letters and a weekend visit with her in the camp "Gaberzee" where she lived with her parents and sister. Her brother was the president of the Jewish survivors Organization in Germany. Rachel was a nice and attractive girl and I kind of liked her. During the weekend that I spent with her in that camp, it became clear to me that she would not leave her family and go with me to America, and I didn't want to leave Evelyn and go to Israel. Rachel's family was going to go to Israel and I decided to cool our relationship off.

Across from Evelyn's apartment lived two sisters, one was married; Ruzia was single. I visited Ruzia many times but really did not think of anything. It was just a matter of spending time. But one day I met at Ruzia's apartment, a girl who I fell in love with immediately. Her name was Regina. She lived with her mother and three brothers. She was not a complete stranger, for she came in several times to the school to inquire about the school progress of her brothers, and because I was the boy's teacher, we met a few times.

Regina was a beautiful girl of almost 18, very charming but we really did not pay any attention to each other at that time. I had to behave very correctly because of my position in school and not until we met at Ruzia's house, did I begin to think about Regina. We began meeting more often, first in the company of her girlfriends, and later alone.

At the time, I taught evening school for young adults and

Regina and her girlfriends attended the class I was teaching, and rumors began to circulate that the teacher and Regina were in love. We began seeing each other more often, listening to each other's stories of the war years.

On our first evening out, we walked inside the camp and then walked out to the Bridge near the camp where we stood looking to the flowing water. We talked much about the war years and our hopes and aspirations for the future. There at the bridge and the flowing river, looking into her smiling eyes, I suddenly realized that I was genuinely in love. It seemed to me that the time had come to settle down, and my feeling was that Regina should be the girl to accompany me through life. I felt that this feeling was mutual and our relation became closer and stronger. We began making plans, and the birth of my nephew, Martin, Evelyn's son, hastened things.

At the Bris, I was to be the one who would hand over the baby for the circumcision, and by Jewish Tradition, I was to be accompanied by a girl who was a close relation, perhaps one destined for marriage. Evelyn and Albert expected me to bring Ruzia, but my plans were already made, and I informed Evelyn the day of the Bris that Regina would be the one, and they accepted.

When we sat at the table to have refreshments, raising my glass in a toast of Mazel-Tov to my sister and brother-in-law, Evelyn made the startling announcement that today is also our engagement, and that Regina and I were planning to get married soon! Since Regina's mother was also present, it was quite a shock to her. Everybody wished us well and the anticipation of a wedding began.

Chapter 40
Regina

My future sister in law, Evelyn, was Stanley's older sister. She had a baby in the camp, and everyone was so excited, again new life and a BOY! I wanted to make a good impression and so I stayed up all night sewing a blanket and putting ribbons and bows on the blanket. Plus, I made curtains for his carriage. They named him Martin and at his bris (six weeks after he was born, because he was jaundiced his circumcision and bris was delayed), Stanley stood up and said, "Since everyone is together and it's a celebration, I have another announcement. Regina and I are getting married.

I didn't know that was what he was planning, we had been dating but I was so young, I never thought about being married! I looked at my mother and she looked at me and we were both shocked. I didn't know anything about life and less than that about being a wife. Everyone started clapping and carrying on. Of course I was happy, but at the same time, surprised.

Regina at about 18 years old

Chapter 41
Stanley

In the meantime, my sister Lillian in New York, began taking steps to bring me to America, but my intention to get married made matters worse, because now it would be somebody else besides me and I didn't know at the time what problems Lillian had at home.

She wrote to me that there were pretty girls in America and that I should not hurry into getting married. But my plans were made already and I informed my sister in the next letter that while appreciating her advice, I put her on notice that on July 1, 1947, Regina and I would be wed.

Now the preparations for the wedding began in earnest. The wedding was to take place in the school, which was not used now because of vacation, and was big enough to accommodate our 125 guests. A wedding gown was no problem, there were several gowns in camp, and all brides used them. As for myself, I borrowed a suit from a friend. My own suit was not suitable for a wedding.

I bought Regina a gold watch as an engagement present and she wore it only for a few days when a little boy climbing in one day through the window to her room, stole it along with some other things. Regina's mother happened to come home and found the boy jumping out the window, notified the police and the boy was taken to the police, but he did not have the watch. I was in Munich that day and when I returned toward evening, Albrt told me the watch was stolen and Regina and I were very upset. Luckly after questioning, the boy led the police to a little tree along a busy path where the watch lay, untouched. It was a happy ending.

During the week before the wedding a German baker came to Regina's apartment to bake all the necessary cakes and help prepare all the food. Before the wedding, Regina went to the Mikvah, as Jewish law required, and I was forbidden to see her before the wedding, which I really ignored! Once of the old ladies next door was really making sure that I don't see Regina, the day before the wedding, but she did not succeed.

Regina's girlfriends travelled to Much and brought a tub full of beautiful, fresh flowers and the brothers, Paul, Johnny and other boys brought in from the town nearby a big wooden barrel of beer, which they rolled on the road some three kilometers, right to the school where the wedding was to be held.

Because there were three weddings that night, Tuesday, July 1, 1947, I told the Rabbi that our wedding was the last one and was to be held about 11 p.m. I was sitting with the men in one room, and Regina was in the big room where the reception was to be held. Through the windows, our school children were peeking in, in an attempt to see their teacher preparing for the wedding. When a light bulb burned out, and I went to replace it where Regina was sitting, I was immediately chased out by the women, who were watching her.

The Chuppa ceremony was held outside in front of the school and the rain which lasted through the day, abruptly stopped, enabling many people to be around, to watch the ceremony, particularly many of the little girls who were bitterly crying, seeing their beloved teacher getting married. I asked the Canto to receipt the traditional prayers in memory of my parents and Regina's father who were murdered by the Nazi's and couldn't see their children getting married. This was a very somber moment in my life, and I barely held back my tears.

After the Chuppa, as we entered the building, the same old lady who prevented me from seeing Regina before the wedding pushed us in a dark room to be alone—a Jewish Tradition. But I switched on the light and kissed my wife and we both joined the guests at the reception.

The prefabricated plywood building across from the school, which we used for many social functions, now served as the dancing hal, where a few of my colleague teachers and one student played in the band. The dancing went on for several hours, and early in the morning, we went to sleep, at a friend's home which was vacated for the night.

Because our one room apartment was not yet ready for us, we stayed with Regina's mother for a week, and then moved to our new 'home'.

*Regina and Stanley's wedding photo, with
Regina's best friend Eva.*

Chapter 42
Regina

Now I was going to be a wife. I barely knew anything about taking care of a house, we hadn't had a house for so long. My mother helped me and taught me about cooking, cleaning, being a dutiful wife, and prepared me for my life ahead. My sister-in-law, who already was married and with a baby was also helpful.

Our wedding was very simple. We got married in the camp, everyone came to celebrate, and some of the young girls were upset that their beloved teacher was being "taken away" from them and getting married! We lived in a small house near my mother and brothers. No real honeymoon, no fancy dress, just simple and surrounded by whatever family we had and new friends.

As life went on in the camp, people began to develop into entrepreneurs. Some learned to trade or barter with the local Germans who were trading on the black market. They would gather their goods and sell or barter with others in a corner of their home. There were no store fronts or shops.

People traded for everything, and I learned how to trade too. Sometimes we traded and got things we didn't understand, like tuna in a can. I never heard of it; I wasn't even sure it was edible! The smell when I opened the can was something I never smelled but another young wife said she tried it and it was edible, so we tried it too. Now looking back, I have to laugh at how naïve I was! And of course, coming from a home where everything was prepared from scratch, and tuna was something we never ate, it was a learning experience and I realized it would be an acquired taste.

Later, when we were in America, I remember sending Jello to Mrs. Mukofsky – the woman that let us stay in her barn and field while we were hiding. I remember my mother saying we needed to give back to her, she was so kind and risked her life to keep us safe. We have so much now that we are in America, as a thank we would send packages to her and her family. Now that we learned what Jello was and we had plenty of it here in America we thought we'd send that over. We boxed up Jello, some clothes and whatever else we could afford to share and send it with a note to enjoy and thanked her again.

A few weeks later we got a note from her, she wrote "Panya (Mrs.) Brottman, we received your package, but I'm sorry we don't understand the pink powder. Are we supposed to eat it like that? Sprinkle it on our food? Is it safe to eat? We appreciate your sending packages but please explain what this is, we will hold onto it until we hear from you.'

I remember seeing this handwritten letter in Polish and reading it with my mother. We laughed and laughed, remembering our own reaction to Jello the first time we saw it!

My mother wrote back right away and explained what it is, how to use it and that it was indeed sweet. My mothers' handwritten letter was mailed back, and we found out in later letters that it was received and understood and that YES, they DID enjoy the Jello!

Chapter 43
Stanley

      Our one room apartment was located in the center of camp, it had a separate bathroom and a special unit for hot water and also a bathtub, which only a few apartments in camp had. We had a bed, closet, and a table with a few chairs, which represented all the furniture. Heat was provided by a small metal stove, wood fired, which also served for cooking. At first, we ate with Regina's mother and brothers, but after a few weeks, we were on our own, and Regina mastered quickly the art of cooking, and became very good at it.

      We did not go on a honeymoon, instead I had to take about 50 children for summer camp some 50 kilometers from Fohrenwald, near lake Starenberg, not far from the Jewish Camp Feldrfling. Here we slept in tents and joined in camp activities, with other youngsters who were also part of this camping site, which was sponsored by the United Nations Relief Organization. I had to struggle being responsible for 50 youngsters near a lake. Regina came twice to visit me at the camp site, and once took a rowboat ride across the lake. On the way back I missed our camp site and wound up rowing the boat 8 kilometers off course, missing lunch and creating panic among my children. I spent 2 weeks with the youngsters in camp and brought all of them home safely.

      Life in camp was interesting, for it was like a small town where most people knew each other, many going through the same experience through the war years and sharing the same goal: to get out of the camp and start a new life. I was in charge of most activities at the school, during and after school. I was involved in staging all school plays, leading the school choir, and because of all that, everybody knew me well and greatly respected me. The children of our school greatly respected the teachers, and Regina got the same respect from the children. Many times, Regina helped out when we had a school play, which was held in the central hall of the camp and was attended by hundreds of residents.

      It was very gratifying to see our Jewish children, who miraculously survived the holocaust, growing up normally, learning, playing, singing and dancing. When I met those children 30 years later at a reunion, many married with children of their own, and later met one of my students who was a general in the Israeli Tank Division, I realized how much did in our little school in Camp Fohrenwald.

Early in 1948, I was hospitalized for two weeks with an attack of bursitis, which I got because I stood in water in our cellar too long. I was advised to take sulfa baths, because also Regina suffered from arthritis in her hands, as a result of many months of hiding in the fields and forest. We spent a month in the famous sanatorium of Bad Vise, Germany, where we took Sulfa baths and had a great time, sort of a delayed honeymoon.

Stanley and Regina on their honeymoon, at the lake where Stanley took his students from camp – they made it their honeymoon too, 1947

Chapter 44
Regina

The Germans in town didn't have a lot either, even though they lived in the country that was led by a killer, in some way, they were just like us, devasted from the war, with little left for them. Cigarettes were a big trading item, and of course everyone got addicted so they were really in demand. Once we got Jello, and literally thought we were supposed to eat it like powder! We had no idea what to do with it and didn't know about refrigerators so what else would you do with pink powder?

I got to be good at bartering; I swapped for wool so I could make a sweater. I may not have known what Jello was, but I knew wool could be used to make a sweater and I had already experienced the winter in barely enough clothes to keep warm, so I was determined to be prepared.

Everything we did, we always kept in our minds, how to not antagonize G-d

Once I needed a bra, it had been about two years since I even owned one. So, my friends Manya and Eva and I went about figuring out how to make one. First, we got some used paper. Then we measured my body, cut out a pattern, then bartered for material. After we got the material, we put the pattern on the fabric and cut! Eventually after much trimming, sewing and adjusting, I had a bra. We were so proud of ourselves for being creative.

There were no clothing stores and I needed at least one or two sweaters. So again, we turned to our creativity. I had some pink wool and a lot of gray wool. I thought about it, talked to my friends and decided to make the bottom gray (since I had more gray than pink) and the top pink. It was the most beautiful sweater ever and I wore it proudly all the time!

Manya was always creative, Eva not so much. We saw Eva about 35 years after the war, she lived in the Miami area. We tracked her down when we were in Florida. She looked old. And said she was not happy with who she married but never had the courage to leave. I felt terrible that as my life turned out to be good.

Camp life was all about trading and being entrepreneurial. I guess after surviving the total insanity of life, being hunted like animals by other humans, and learning how to be cunning, secretive and sly, being entrepreneurial was easy.

Life in these displaced persons camps showed the true cost of war and the resilience of the human spirit. People flocked there from all over Europe and beyond. Those who had survived the war and Holocaust were trying to find family and friends to reclaim a sense of unity and begin rebuilding their lives. Slowly, people ceased to plan their lives around the expectation of hunger and danger. Pageants and religious services were performed. A camp newspaper was published, and children resumed their education.

The American Generals George Patton and Dwight Eisenhauer both visited the camp to assess our situation firsthand. Though I did not see this with my own eyes, I understand that Eisenhauer wept for our suffering, while Patton merely spat on the floor.

It was in this camp that a semblance of normalcy and comfort gradually returned. Over the many years that followed, people would notice how calmly I was able to relate my experiences in conversation. To begin to understand what we went through, one must realize that anyone who allowed the experience to affect them emotionally would be unable to function and survive. The trauma of the experience quickly forced us to become numb and fearless so we could do what was necessary. It also left us with a sense of wariness and mistrust that lingered for years. It became part of who we were.

We never lost our gratitude to the people who had helped us. After the war we corresponded with many of these brave individuals and tried to assist them in their own troubles whenever we could. One such instance involved the family of the farmer who had been beaten to death for allowing us to hide in his basement. The farmer's son was in the Polish army and lost both his legs fighting the Nazis. He contacted us after the war and explained that he needed money to purchase a special vehicle for transportation. We sent him the money and he was able to use the vehicle to commute to work and move on with his life.

At one point, Mrs. Mukofski sent us a letter explaining that someone in their family was very sick and in need of antibiotics. They asked if we could obtain the medicine they needed, which was very rare in Poland at that time. We were able to help them get the prescription, allowing her family member to recover from his illness.

Stanley's family had suffered greatly during the war. Like many other people, Stanley had returned to the region to pick up the pieces of his life and try to find his family. Stanley and I gradually spent time together outside of the school and then alone. Some of Stanley's female students had a crush on him and wept when we became engaged.

Stanley and Regina on their way to America

Chapter 45
Stanley

By now, my sister Lillian was arranging for us the necessary paper to bring us to America, and during the summer of 1948, we were called to the CIA for investigation. This was the procedure to receive a visa to come to the US. After the CIA appointment we had to wait to be called to the American Consulate in Munich.

In November 1948, after a German dentist pulled one of my teeth and left the root in my mouth, I had to undergo surgery to remove the root. It was done by the surgeon, with anesthesia and my class was waiting in the corridor of the small hospital. The girls cried and were relieved when they saw me come out within the hour, although slightly groggy. Later in the day, the mailman brought us a letter from the American Consulate in Munich, to come to the office for the Visa. We were overjoyed and within a few days we went to the consulate.

Evelyn and Albert were also called to the consulate, and while we were already assigned to a transport from Brcmen, the port of departure, Evelyn's papers were not ready. In order to travel together, we had to postpone our departure for the next transport. The packing was not a big problem, we did not have much. We also did not know what we should take along. We did buy from a German lady a 12-piece China set, which we packed in a wooden box, which Albert made in the wood shop. We also had another smaller box and an aluminum suitcase, in which we packed everything we had. That was approximately what we owned at the time, plus $50 American money.

At the end of January 1949, we left camp Fohrenwald, after living there for four years. It was not easy to say goodbye to the many friends that we made. For Evelyn and me, it was especially hard to leave the school, which we helped function since its beginning in 1945, and the hundreds of children that we had educated and seen grow up.

Regina's mother and brothers were also awaiting papers for

America, and although we had to leave them behind, we were confident that they would soon join us.

Camp Fohrenwald was our home for four years, our second home after our parents' home was destroyed by Nazi Germany and our family murdered. As we boarded our bus to leave the camp, there were tears in our eyes; not tears of sorrow, but tears of joy, that finally once again our status will no longer be classified "stateless." We were being given a chance to become a proud citizen of the United States, which opened its gates to the tired and the poor to the stateless refugees of that terrible war.

Our destination was now the Funk Kaserne, a complex of German military barracks which served as a transitional camp for all immigrants to the US and other countries. Conditions here were not "ideal" but, knowing that it was only a temporary stay, it did not matter. Besides during our years as refugees, we were used to it and took everything in stride. We spent about two weeks going through all the formalities and health check-ups, before proceeding to the port of embarkment. Finally, we were taken by train to Bremerhaven, in North Germany, to wait for our ship.

Here we were again housed in military barracks and poor conditions. There was plenty of food, but we had to sleep on the floor and on our baggage, amongst thousands of people, all waiting. Each day, people were called to the American authorities to check again their papers and get assigned a ship for America. Evelyn and Albert's papers were processed but ours were not. We advised them to go, while we waited for ours to clear, which came a week later. We were assigned to the SS General Muir and waited impatiently for the departure.

This was an American troop transport ship and the accommodations were not the very best. Men and women were separated in big rooms, and we slept in three-tier hanging beds, each room containing several hundred people. We cleaned the room ourselves and maintained the proper discipline.

As our ship left the shores of Germany, we looked for the last time at Europe, and with tears in our eyes, recalled that in this European soil we left behind the remains of our parents, brothers, sisters, entire families which the Nazi's murdered and whose graves were not even known.

Upon entering the Atlantic the next morning, many people became seasick, among them Regina. It was a pity to see people barely able to walk and not wanting to take anything in their mouth. That lasted seven days, and while at first there were lines to the dining room, they gradually shrunk because so many refused to eat. I was ok and even ate some of Regina's food.

Our ship carried 1,500 people, among them Jews, Ukrainians, Poles and others. Much time was spent on dec, where we talked and sang in Russian and Polish. This was the only form of entertainment for almost eleven days. As we neared the Gulf Stream, the weather became very stormy and everyone was ordered off the deck and the doors shut because the waves were high. It was so scary to be in the middle of the stormy ocean, bur out ship was big and rode the waves safely, coming ever closer to the shores of the USA.

We entered the Hudson River on the eleventh day, toward evening and had to say aboard till the next morning. It was beautiful to see the shores of Brooklyn and Manhattan with the thousands of lights shimmering in the dark and above all knowing that in the morning, we would step down on the shores of America and begin a new life in the land of the free.

Standing there that evening, of March 19, 1949, on the deck of a US troop carrier in the New York Harbor, I tried to reflect in my mind of all that happened to me during the last eight years since I left my home in Kostopol, Russia. Beginning with June 22, 1941, I walked hundreds of kilometers, travelled perhaps about 10,000 kilometers by train, lived among various people in different countries, crossed secretly four borders, and finally made it across the Atlantic to the golden land, the United States of America.

I knew that in the morning, I would meet my sister Lillian, whom I had not seen in 10 years, and I wondered what she would be like now and what kind of life she has in America.

Chapter 46
Regina

We came to America with $50 and a tin suitcase. We had no idea how to get around or what to do, so we did what a lot of other immigrants did, we got any job, so we could survive and figure it out.

One day, we were taking the subway and somehow, we got separated! Stanley got on the subway, but I missed it. I never saw subways in my life, I grew up in a small town, and then hiding and then DP camp. The ship over was more than I could ever imagine but now subways. I learned a little about how they work but without Stanley I was really stuck. A police officer somehow explained that I should go to the next stop and wait for Stanley there. So, I did, I wasn't sure what else to do. But of course, Stanley came back to where I was. In the end we figured it out, mostly because he was in Russia during the war, and had seen subways before.

When I was pregnant, I was walking down the street with Stanley, and I was so thirsty! I was probably seven months pregnant but needed some water. We passed a bar and so I went in, asked for a glass of water and drank it down quickly. The men at the bar almost passed out when they saw a pregnant woman walk in and drink what they thought was VODKA!

Stanley's brother-in-law encouraged us to buy a chicken farm in Connecticut. Our property was in the middle of nowhere. But we had a house and felt somewhat safe. Our property had a state line through it so part of our property was in Rhode Island and part in Connecticut. That's when we found others from the "old country." They were easily identifiable. They had an accent, and many had numbers tattooed on their arms. These were the numbers the Nazi's gave each person they took into the camps.

We eventually moved to New Jersey to be closer to my mother. We moved to Lakewood, where we would eventually settle, where my mother and her new husband lived. We raised chickens, had three children, and found an entire community of other survivors, all marked by the numbers on their arms and the look in their eyes that only a survivor can recognize. The numbers on their arms were a constant reminder of what they survived and a constant reminder that it did happen – inconceivable as it was. These numbers serve as proof!

Having finally settled down, we were ready to work and make money from our thousands of chickens. Our children were old enough to take on the responsibilities involved in helping us run our farm and sell eggs to local customers. The children lived carefree and without fear, playing in the woods and field behind the chicken coops. In this manner, the years passed peacefully.

***

My brothers did well. Johnny went on to become an accomplished soccer player and was recruited to play professionally in Canada. At one point he broke his leg in a game but recovered and continued to play. Eventually he settled down to live in the US and coached soccer. Later he worked as a cloth cutter, slicing material for slacks and other garments. Jack joined the U.S. Army and worked on maps as a draftsman. Johnny was popular with my children and grandchildren, who considered their uncle a "badass."

Paul continued to excel in school. He only struggled with learning English. At one point, the school contacted our mother and invited her to meet to discuss Paul's education. My mother, who had come to anticipate catastrophe, assumed her son was being thrown out of school and begged that he be shown mercy. It took her some time to realize the actual purpose of the meeting was to praise Paul's academic skills and suggest special courses to improve his English.

Chapter 47
Regina

It was not until the 1970s that I began speaking publicly about my family's experiences during the war. The survivors almost never spoke about the war or the Holocaust in its immediate aftermath. Everyone had their own story and their own pain to deal with in their own way. I could not exist and raise a family if I could not put what I went through out of my mind.

My brothers were too young to remember much. Jack remembered almost nothing, and Paul's memories were sketchy. Johnny remained happy-go-lucky and didn't seem to reflect much on the past. My mother never fully conquered the English language. My daughter Paula always encouraged me to speak publicly and share my stories with others.

As organizations began to express an interest in the subject, and I visited schools to share my story with the students, and even sewed exact replicas of the armbands and yellow stars we were forced to wear so that my audiences would have visual aids to help them grasp what I was describing. My grandson once asked if we had to wear armbands to bed. My story was a somewhat different than the story told by people who survived the concentration camps.

Some of the venues where I spoke included Rider College and Metuchen High School, as well as interfaith religious services and various synagogues. I even spoke to my granddaughter Shelby's fifth grade class.

Many audience members wrote letters to me. One high school student told me that although he had read about the Holocaust and seen films on the subject, he never truly believed it until he was face to face with a real person who had lived through it.

I also met and corresponded with many other people who had survived the Nazi occupations or served in the Allied armies. One of my neighbors in Lakewood was also a Holocaust survivor. He had escaped from a Nazi concentration camp where he was tasked with loading the dead bodies of other prisoners into the ovens, and shared photos to prove it.

Stanley later corresponded and met with several of his former students from the displaced persons' camp and gained a new appreciation for the hope and healing he brought to their lives in the aftermath of the Holocaust. One of his students had even gone on to become a general in the Israeli tank forces.

I never returned to Europe. In the years since coming to America I have travelled to Israel, Canada, and Mexico, but you couldn't pay me to return to Poland. All I really have are bad memories of my home. I try to focus on happier things.

While there have been many dreadful dictators in the history of the world, I find no comparison in the news today to what occurred in the Nazi concentration camps. Hitler was an insecure little man with a talent for public speaking and a gang of true hoodlums around him. I feel the world learned how low a human being can sink, but I wonder if only the people who truly met this atrocity face to face understand it.

There is an expression in Europe that goes, "You should never be subjected to how much you can endure." Some people who endured the Holocaust lost their faith in God, but I still feel grateful to the Almighty. The more I think about it, the more I think some things are destined. You can plan and toil but if something is meant to be, it is going to be. I also saw meaning in the hardship and loss we endured in our later years. Stanely and some of my other family members had cancer and spent time in hospitals, but when their time came, all died at home.

Though I cannot claim to understand God's plan, I believe everything and everyone in this world is part of a greater purpose. Everyone must accept their destiny and work with what God gives them as best they can. We can achieve this by doing as my mother did, by keeping God in our hearts.

Chapter 48
Stanley

Life in Leah's home was not ideal, and we wanted to get our own place. After arrangements with the NY Organization to Help Refugees, we moved into a furnished room in Brooklyn. We had no mortgage, no car, no insurance and we just had enough to get food.

I began looking for work, walking Coney Island Avenue every day, getting more and more frustrated. Then I heard that a shoe factory in Brooklyn needed workers, so I went to inquire about a job. It was Langerman Shoe Company, as I looked around in the lobby a man asked me what I was looking for. I said Mr. Langerman. The man sighed and said, "Mr. Langerman has been dead for 5 years but if you're looking for a job, come with me."

Mr. Spiegel was the boss and was very kind. He called the foreman and informed him that I was a holocaust survivor and to find me a job. After the Foreman insisted that there were no jobs Mr. Spiegel hit the desk with his fist and said, "This man will be here to work tomorrow at 8:00 AM and you'll find him a job." I was incredibly grateful to Mr. Spiegel.

Soon I was able to get Regina a job at the factory and we both made $60/week and for the time we were content.

But David, Leah's husband, was steering us into buying a farm and going into the poultry business with him. After traveling to Connecticut to look at a farm and visiting friends who owned a farm and seemed to be happy, the idea was starting to appeal to us. We met a representative from the Jewish Agricultural Society who promised to help us find a farm with the little money that we did have.

Chapter 49
Regina

In July 1949, my mother and brothers Jack and Paul came from Germany. It was incredible to see them again. Cousins in the Bronx helped my mother and brothers settled into an apartment and it was wonderful to be able to see them regularly.

Johnny was in Canada. He had left with a group of children and was now living in Montreal. Johnny went on to become an accomplished soccer player and was recruited to play professionally in Canada. At one point he broke his leg in a game but recovered and continued to play. Eventually he settled down and moved to live in the US and coached soccer. Later he worked as a cloth cutter, slicing material for slacks and other garments. Johnny was popular with my children and grandchildren, who considered their uncle a tough guy, a bit wild and full of adventure.

Jack and Paul attended school and later, Jack joined the U.S. Army and worked on maps as a draftsman.

Paul continued to excel in school. He only struggled with learning English. At one point, the school contacted our mother and invited her to meet to discuss Paul's education. My mother, who had come to anticipate catastrophe, assumed her son was being thrown out of school and begged that he be shown mercy. It took her some time to realize the actual purpose of the meeting was to praise Paul's academic skills and suggest special courses to improve his English.

Stanley's brother-in-law was still trying to encourage us to buy a chicken farm in Connecticut. But we still didn't have money and more than that, to settle on a farm, Stanley had to learn to drive.

Chapter 50
Stanley

I had to take driving lessons! I took lessons in Brooklyn for $4/hour and learned on Coney Island Avenue. I was very scared at first, but shortly I got the hang of it. The instructor never asked me for a permit, and I never knew I needed one. When I came for the road test, the instructor asked me for my permit, and I explained I didn't have one, he sent me straight to the Motor Vehicle Office. I passed the written test but couldn't see the small letters on the eye exam. They told me I needed glasses, which I had from Munich and only used once. The next day I returned to the office with the permit and my glasses and the instructor almost fainted saying "I drove with you without a permit AND without glasses!"

The fall brought news that a farm was available near the town of Danielson, Connecticut and we could buy it with the little bit of money we had. Albert and I took a bus to Willimantic, Connecticut to meet Mr. Miller from the Jewish Agricultural Society who would show us the farm.

We already felt so far from New York, but somehow this remote area felt familiar to us from our upbringing, and we felt safe. The farm was located on a dirt road in the town of Foster, Rhode Island, consisting of 35 acres of fields and pine trees with 5 acres of the town belonging to Sterling, Connecticut. The house was small and there were old and empty chicken coops. Most important was the price - $10,000. Between a few loans and money we saved, we told Mr. Miller that we liked it, and we were ready to begin a new life as farmers.

We returned to New York to begin planning. By now Regina was in the early months of her pregnancy and we were anxious to get out of NY and to our own home.

Chapter 51
Regina

Our property was in the middle of nowhere. But we had a house and felt somewhat safe. Our property had a state line through it, so part of our property was in Rhode Island and part in Connecticut.

Evely and Albert along with their son Martin were living with us in a house that was really too small for all of us, but we got busy organizing things and bringing to house into order and somehow, we made it work.

We quickly realized that we were the first Jewish family to live in Foster and the nearest family like ours was 3 miles away.

That's when we found others from the "old country." They were easily identifiable. They had an accent, and many had numbers tattooed on their arms. These were the numbers the Nazi's gave each person they took into the camps.

First home in Connecticut, a chicken farm with half the property in Rhode Island.

Chapter 52
Stanley

We were the first Jewish families in the town of Foster, RI, population 1200. The nearest Jewish family were the Shatzmans who were poultry farmers 3 miles away from us and other Jewish farmers lived even farther. We learned that the shopping town was Danielson, Connecticut, just 6 miles away and here we learned that there were several Jewish families, some farmers and newcomers. Most of the new farmers were, like us, survivors of the war in Europe and we shared our stories and common problems.

The Feed Company, in Danielson was owned by two Jewish brothers, who were very religious and promised us credit. One of the brothers, Charles Gordon said that with God's help, we will make a living and be able to pay him back.

Next, we arranged to buy baby chicks, on credit and the job of preparing the coops began.

Chapter 53
Regina

We were told the coops should be very clean to prevent disease to the baby chicks. So, Evelyn and I scrubbed and swept the cement floors clean of any dust and washed the cement by hand. All windows were cleaned spotless with spic-n-span and the building was sprayed with disinfectants.

Our neighbor and former owner of our farm, Mr. Neimi, and another old Finish farmer, came over to show us how to operate the brooding stoves, under which the baby chicks will be housed for several weeks, and how to maintain them, giving us instructions for how to care for the chicks. Afterall, this was our first try in business and we certainly had no room for failure.

Soon, 5000 baby chicks were delivered and after several sleepless nights watching the baby chicks first days and nights, we knew what to do and we started to feel settled.

During Passover, I started to have what seemed like labor pains but turned out to be a false alarm. But on Friday, May 11, 1950, the pain became steadier and more unbearable, and Stanley took me to Day Kimbal Hospital in Putnam, Connecticut, about 16 miles from the farm.

Chapter 54
Stanley

I took Regina to the Hospital in Putnam and was told to wait, that perhaps in a few hours I will be a daddy. Her water broke that evening, and they were sure the baby would be born soon. About 11 o'clock, Dr. Chartier came over and told me to go home, that nothing was happening and that I should come back in the morning.

The next day, they were still waiting and the doctor kept reassuring me that he was doing everything he could do as if it was his own wife (he had 12 children).

Finally, Sunday, the second day in the hospital, they tried to induce labor and with the medication they gave her Regina was completely out of it. She didn't know what was happening and thankfully I was able to stay with her in the delivery room.

Finally, by that evening, Regina was still groggy from the medication and my eyes were filled with tears, we welcomed our son, Morris into the world. It was May 14, 1950.

Chapter 55
Regina

The birth of our son was very difficult for me. I didn't feel like the doctors or nurses understood me, I was afraid and then with the medication, I was so groggy.

But here he was, our baby boy. Morris Zektzer, born, May 14, 1950. I was a mother.

The day after Morris was born, I saw that there was something wrong with his foot. It was twisted around.

The doctor assured us that it was nothing and it would straighten out, but I was worried and thought if this needed medical attention, how would we pay for that? We had no insurance and very little money.

I came home and began planning for the 'bris'. The baby was named Morris Alan, after my father Mojshe. The Mohel, who was a new American from Hungary, a holocaust survivor as well, said that a friend of his is an orthopedic doctor in New York and he would certainly take care of Morris' foot. But his fee and the schedule he suggested was impossible. We returned home and didn't know what to do.

Luckily, the Rhode Island State Traveling nurse stopped for a visit and suggested an orthopedic doctor in Providence, 25 miles away. Dr. Sage was fantastic and helped put Morris in a cast, gave us a reasonable schedule for appointments and only charged us $8. He was very interested in us because we were new Americans and holocaust survivors, and he liked to discuss the Bible with us.

Chapter 56
Stanley

Over the next couple of years, we settled into farm life, gaining experience and we started to feel more settled. Our community expanded as more and more holocaust survivors came to town and the Jewish farming community grew to one of the largest in Connecticut. Regina was pregnant again and we felt like we were building a good life.

Now expecting our second child, on the morning of November 9, 1954, I drove Regina to the hospital in Putnam and at 4:00 p.m., Regina called me to say that it was a boy and that everything is fine.

Regina and I were happy that everything was ok and made all preparations to have a nice Bris for Marvin. We named him after my father- Mordechai, Reuven (my grandfather on my father's side).

Late in 1955, Regina was pregnant, and we hoped now that it would be a girl! But this time we had to switch doctors, to Norwich, Connecticut, some 35 miles away. We were told this doctor was one of the best in the area and we were sure that he would do the best job.

On May 26, 1956, the pain started, and we went to the hospital. I left Regina there to return home to watch the other two children. But by 6:00 p.m. there was no call about her progress. I called the hospital and was told that Regina was doing nothing. Knowing from experience that a prolonged delivery may be hazardous to the baby, I again called the hospital at 8:00 pm and was told that she is still doing nothing. I asked to speak to the doctor, but he was home and they refused to give his home telephone number.

I was outraged and threatened the head nurse that I would hold her personally responsible if I was not given the doctor's telephone number. Finally, the doctor called me from his home and said that she is doing very little so I asked him what he was doing at home? He realized that I was very upset when I told him that I'll hold him responsible if he would not go immediately to the hospital. He assured me that he would do just that and withing 90 minutes, Regina called saying 'It's a girl!'

We named her Paula Dina, after my mother and with the addition of this little girl, we realized we needed more room, and began thinking about remodeling the house.

The Zektzer, Brottman and Elbaum families in America. Left to right, Stanley and Regina Zektzer. Johnny, Clara and Paul Brottman. Evelyn and Albert Elbaum. Front row, Jack Brottman and the baby is Martin Elbaum.

Chapter 57
Regina

I was now expecting our second child and with the farm being busy, I was wondering how I would handle a second child.

When the pain started I knew it was time to go and after almost an entire day of labor, the baby was born, and it was a boy! The doctors and nurses thought I was crazy as I screamed immediately that I wanted to see the baby's feet! I was so afraid that this baby would have the same issue Morris had, but when I saw him and his feet were perfect, I cried with relief and joy at having another boy!

It wasn't long after that that I found myself pregnant, again! I was barely managing life with 2 boys and the farm, but we always believed in bringing new life into the world and this time I was hoping it was a girl.

Our doctor had a heart attack and so we had to go to a new doctor, in Norwich, Connecticut. It felt like I was too far to drive, and I was not sure I wanted to go to another doctor, but we had no choice.

We were busy with the farm and found ourselves doing well. Throughout my pregnancy I was working side-by-side with Stanley as we continued to build our life on the farm, with the community and with the Synagogue.

It was May and the weather was starting to get warmer, and Morris and Marvin were typical boys always into something. When the pain started, I told Stanley it was time to go. Arriving at the hospital I felt a little better prepared but as the day went on and not much was happening, I started to get anxious. Stanley had to return to the farm to look after the boys and the only thing on my mind was will the babies feet be straight.

When evening came and the pains got worse, the doctor arrived and before too long, I delivered the baby, and they told me "It's a girl!" By now the nurses realized my fear about the baby's feet and so they brought her to me and showed me her feet were straight and I was so happy to have a girl!

Regina and Stanley's children, from left Marvin, Morris, and Paula

Chapter 58
Stanley

In the spring of 1958, we decided to take a trip to Detroit, Michigan where our Aunt Ziesel (the Seargent), and her daughter lived.

On the way, we stopped in Lakewood to leave our children with Regina's mother and drove to Detroit. Aunt Ziesel and her daughter were surprised to see a newcomer to America being able to find their way to Detroit by car and above all so quickly Americanized. Going home we drove on the Canadian side of Niagara Falls, where we spent a day and returned to Lakewood, NJ to pick up our kids and return home.

Later in 1961, our lucky break came when a family from Passaic, NJ, came to our area, looking to buy a farm, and stopped at our place.

This was our chance to make a change, move to a new area and start all over again. According to the Jewish tradition, a change of place also brings a change of luck, and we hoped for better luck.

Jack came with Paul's egg truck and took our furniture and most of the bigger boxes, leaving only small things which I was able to take in the car.

The Synagogue threw a farewell party for us and the entire community and friends from the neighboring towns were invited. We were presented by the Synagogue with a silverplated tea set and all expressed regret that we were leaving. In my speech I recalled the first years of our settling in the area, the organization of this Jewish community and the camaraderie of the famers in those early years. We hoped to stay in contact with the Danielson Jewish Community where we were among the organizers and members for 12 years.

When the morning of our departure came, I was heartbroken. On the one hand, we were happy to get out of there and make our home in a larger Jewish community and new possibilities, but on the other hand, there was sadness, because we were leaving behind our first home and property that we owned and where all our children were born and grew up, during the past 12 years.

True, we were financially better off now, walking away from the property with $30,000, $29,000 more than the $1,000 which we began in 1950 but above all was the reward of having raised on the farm, three beautiful children, hoping to give them a better chance in a new home at another place.

We said good-bye to the new owners with tears stuck in the throat and with the family crammed in the loaded car, we drove off on the way to Lakewood, New Jersey, for a temporary stay with Regina's mother, while looking into what to do next.

Chapter 59
Regina

We took a trip to Detroit to visit some relatives and thought we could leave the children with my mother in Lakewood. Being young and needing to get away by ourselves, we felt safe leaving the children with my mother, she lived on a farm, and we thought the children would feel at home there.

On our return to New Jersey, we passed through Niagara Falls, I've never seen such a site, it was incredible! But I missed the children, and I was ready to go home. When we arrived, my mother had cut Paula's hair so short, she was crying that grandma had cut her hair, but the boys were fine and happy to see us.

A few years later, a family from New Jersey came to our area, looking to buy a farm, and when they saw our farm and how well we had developed it, they were interested in buying our property and we thought this is a great opportunity we needed to consider.

It was bittersweet, and the farewell party the Synagogue threw for us drew people from the entire community. In our hearts we knew it was time to go and look for the next phase of our lives, but at the same time, we were sad to leave all of our close friends and the home we had made for all these years.

Chapter 60
Stanley

Because there were still a couple of months until the end of the school year, we enrolled the children into Lakewood schools, while we began exploring what to do

We also looked into buying another farm in Lakewood, which at the time was very reasonable, and the properties were in very good shape. We were looking for a nice home on the farm and we found one in Lakewood, right in town, asking price was $36,000. We were interested!

Then, one evening my cousin Morris, in Los Angeles, called, suggesting that we come out and perhaps settle there. While we were still undecided what to do, we waited until the children finished school, then in June 1962, we made the decision to drive to Los Angeles and try our luck there. This was a drive of some 3000 miles, and it took courage, but we thought we've survived so much, we can do this too.

Driving, we realized America is a BIG country and the road ahead of us felt like it would never end.

On the 5th day driving, we reached Tucson, Arizona, where we stopped for a couple of days to visit with friends who had a farm near us in Connecticut and were now living in Tucson. Without air conditioning in the car, it was hot, and the children's crayons began to melt as they lay on the back window. Lucky for us, the car performed well and the water bag that we carried in front on the bumper was not needed. When we emerged from the desert, and reached the California Freeway, we were like in a new world!

To drive on a Freeway in California after emerging from the desert and the little traffic that we had was an experience onto itself. With 6 lanes of traffic in each direction, you had to be VERY alert. To top it all off, it was about 4-5:00 p.m., when the rush hour began, and it was very crowded. We were overwhelmed with the cars and the traffic but finally after about 90 miles on the Freeway, we reached Hollywood Avenue and the home of my cousin Morris.

He had an idea of going into business with me in photo services, which did not appeal to me but we decided to stay and explore other possibilities.

We explored the options of buying a liquor store, parking lot downtown Losa Angeles and a small market all of which presented in our opinion a great risk with the $30,000 cash. We probably did not understand the value of property at the time, and what it would be in the future.

For a trial, I worked with Morris in his Kodak Lab and soon found that this was not profitable business which was on the verge of bankruptcy. When Marvin asked me for a loan of $4,000, I thought it was time to move on. After 5 weeks in Los Angeles, and not finding something concrete to do, we decided to return east and probably settle in Lakewood, NJ.

Chapter 61
Regina

Driving to California we quickly realized just how big America is. We stopped at places we thought the children would enjoy and save money and kept to ourselves by stopping at roadside stops to have a few sandwiches I had packed and at night we'd find a motel with a pool so the children could play and cool off.

Staying with Stanley's cousins was good as we didn't know our way around and they took good care to show us the way to get around. I've never seen a place like California, it was an entirely new world to me, and I wasn't sure if we would stay there or return to New Jersey.

After a few weeks, we decided that California wasn't really for us, and we started to head back to New Jersey and considered looking for a farm in Lakewood where we could be near my mother and brothers and return to a life we knew.

On the way home, Stanely got pulled over for speeding and had to appear in court. We were scared at what this could mean, and I tried to keep calm so the children wouldn't be scared. But memories of the world we left in Poland came rushing back and I prayed silently to get out of this situation and get back to New Jersey.

Finally we were free to go and on our way but now it was getting dark and I was scared and just wanted to be in a safe place for the night and anxious to leave this place.

Chapter 62
Stanley

Within a few days, we were back in New Jersey and now it was approaching fall, and the children would be returning to school in Lakewood.

We turned back to negotiating to buy the farm, which we saw before we left for California. It seemed to us to be the best buy because the house was a new brick house, and the chicken coops were very good. There was about 10 acres of land and above all it was right in town. Lakewood had a nice Jewish Community, where I also could teach in one of the Hebrew schools. The price was now $38,000 because there were now other buyers who were interested.

In January 1963, we became the owners of the new farm in Lakewood!

Chaya and her second husband Samuel Koplowitz. She met him through a friend in the Bronx and decided to get married and move to a chicken farm in Lakewood.

Now it was time to start really working after 9 months of rest. We had to clean the coops, buy chickens, and get into operations. Above all it was time to earn some money.

It was now 13 years since we bought our first property in the newly adopted Land, and now it was 1963 and we had a new acquired home in Lakewood. Our children have grown, and we got a bit older and perhaps wiser. We took on new responsibilities and we were determined to meet the challenge.

Chapter 63
Regina

We returned from California and decided to settle in Lakewood to be my mother and her new husband and to settle in a community where others from the "old country" lived.

We bought a farm, bought chickens and started a new life, using our experience from our farm in Rhode Island we got busy working hard to start making money from our thousands of chickens. Our children were old enough to take on the responsibilities involved in helping us run our farm and sell eggs to local customers. The children lived carefree and without fear, playing in the woods and field behind the chicken coops.

We raised our three children, continued to farm and found an entire community of survivors, all marked by the numbers on their arms and the look in their eyes that only a survivor can recognize. The numbers on their arms were a constant reminder of what they survived and a constant reminder that it did happen – inconceivable as it was. These numbers serve as proof!

***

It was not until the 1970s that I began speaking publicly about my family's experiences during the war. The survivors almost never spoke about the war or the Holocaust in its immediate aftermath. Everyone had their own story and their own pain to deal with in their own way. I could not exist and raise a family if I could not put what I went through out of my mind.

My brothers were too young to remember much. Jack remembered almost nothing, and Paul's memories were sketchy. Johnny remained happy-go-lucky and didn't seem to reflect much on the past. My mother never fully conquered the English language. My daughter Paula always encouraged me to speak publicly and share my stories with others.

As organizations began to express an interest in the subject, I visited schools to share my story with the students, and even sewed exact replicas of the armbands and yellow stars we were forced to wear so that my audiences would have visual aids to help them grasp what I was describing. My grandson once asked if we had to wear armbands to bed.

My story was a somewhat different than the story told by people who survived the concentration camps.

Some of the venues where I spoke included Rider College and Metuchen High School, as well as interfaith religious services and various synagogues. I even spoke to my granddaughter Shelby's fifth grade class. And, every year for over 20 years I spoke at my daughter-in-law's High School history class, where Holocaust studies became part of the curriculum.

Many audience members wrote letters to me. One high school student told me that although he had read about the Holocaust and has seen films on the subject, he never truly believed it until he was face to face with a real person who had lived through it.

I also met and corresponded with many other people who had survived the Nazi occupations or served in the Allied armies. One of my neighbors in Lakewood was also a Holocaust survivor. He had escaped from a Nazi concentration camp where he was tasked with loading the dead bodies of other prisoners into the ovens, and shared photos to prove it.

Stanley later corresponded and met with several of his former students from the displaced persons' camp and gained a new appreciation for the hope and healing he brought to their lives in the aftermath of the Holocaust. One of his students had even gone on to become a general in the Israeli tank forces.

I never returned to Europe. In the years since coming to America I have travelled to Israel, Canada, and Mexico, but you couldn't pay me to return to Poland. All I really have are bad memories of my home. I try to focus on happier things.

While there have been many dreadful dictators in the history of the world, I find no comparison in the news today to what occurred in the Nazi concentration camps. Hitler was an insecure little man with a talent for public speaking and a gang of true hoodlums around him. I feel the world learned how low a human being can sink, but I wonder if only the people who truly met this atrocity face to face understand it.

There is an expression in Europe that goes, "You should

never be subjected to how much you can endure." Some people who endured the Holocaust lost their faith in God, but I still feel grateful to the Almighty. The more I think about it, the more I think some things are destined, it's fate. You can plan and toil but if something is meant to be, it is going to be. I also saw meaning in the hardship and loss we endured in our later years. Stanely and some of my other family members had cancer and spent time in hospitals, but when their time came, all died at home.

***

Though I cannot claim to understand God's plan, I believe everything and everyone in this world is part of a greater purpose and a larger plan than any of us can imagine. Everyone must accept their destiny and work with what God gives them as best they can.

We can achieve this by doing as my mother did, trusting that there is a divine plan, and that fate will guide us all to where we need to be. We were saved by the grace of God, by good people who risked the lives to protect us and by my mother's unwavering determination to never let any of us go, no matter what. She was in many ways, a lioness, always protecting her kids, even when we were adults. And to this day, I say "God works in mysterious ways"

Regina's 75th birthday party with her brothers, right to left, Paul, Jack, amd Johnny

I Long
a poem written by Stanley Zektzer

I long for my home, and the small shtetl where I made my first
steps
Where there live generations of nice Jews
Who with wisdom created a world.
I long for the streets, paved with cobble stone
with Jewish homes and fences around
Where children played without fear
Running all over town.
I long for my garden, the trees and flowers
who grew by the side
the cellar often with water
Especially when the snow melted around Passover
I long for my shul, the old one
Where my father and grandfather were Cantors
And women upstairs were asking what the Cantor was singing
how can we forget the Sabbath delight
to see Jews walk by the river
I long, knowing no one survived
from such a community, rich and poor.
I know it's only a vision
the appears in my thoughts, for a moment
The truth is that I'm only a dreamer
Because what was destroyed, will never be again